# Beginners Guide to Palmistry

# Contents

# Introduction

Many people are fascinated by palmistry, and wonder how the lines in your hand can possibly show so much about not only your past and present but also your future life. Moreover, the lines on your hands are constantly changing, even though only very slightly, as you progress through life, and this is why palmists say that it is best to have readings done every six months.

Traditionally associated with gipsy bands who helped to spread its popularity, palmistry is still widely associated with travellers, but many people, from all walks of life, practise the art and have an interest in learning more about it.

## The History of Palmistry

Palmistry is possibly the oldest form of character reading, first appearing in Chinese history more than two thousand years ago. Classical Greek literature is full of references to divination using the hand. Anaxagoras taught and practised palmistry in 423 BC, and Aristotle was one of many ancient Greeks who regularly studied the science stating 'The hand is the organ of organs, the active agent of the passive powers of the entire system'. In the fifteenth century Hartlieb and Cockles wrote widely on the subject and during the next century, many books appeared in various European languages.  Then palmistry seemed to suffer a decline in popularity, until it was brought back to the public's attention in the middle of the nineteenth century by d'Arpentigny and Desbarroles and gradually became popular once again.

## What you can learn from the hands

Although it is true that the lines on our hands show many things about our character, our health, our mental and emotional natures, relationships, talents and longings, palmistry is the study of the hand in its entirety, not just the lines and marks on its surface.

It is quite easy to look at people's hands without them being aware of your interest, and you can learn a lot from this apparently casual observation. You can look at hands in your own time, in any place; it isn't always necessary to ask to look at the palms to get useful information.

Look at someone near you now. Are they standing with their hands open (if so, they will probably be open sort of people), or with clenched fists (this person is secretive and careful with money)? Do they walk with their arms swinging? They will probably be energetic people if they do. Are their arms just hanging limply as they walk? These people are indecisive. Fidgety people are easy to spot, as are those serene people who walk with their hands gently clasped in front of them. There is so much fun you can have just by observing people without even looking specifically at their hands.

## The Astrological Connection

Those of you interested in astrology will notice as you progress through this book that many astrological terms are used, Mounts of Jupiter, Mercury, Line of Mars etc., and this is not surprising, as astrology and palmistry have been linked for many centuries. Each finger is associated with a planet - the base of the thumb with Venus, the outer edge of the palm with the moon. It was originally thought that the planets influenced the make-up of the hands. However, it is not necessary to understand astrology to look at palmistry in its own right, and indeed, many modern palmists have given up the idea that the planets are linked with the hands. It is, in my opinion, however, something that is not without foundation, and perhaps new schools of palmistry will come back to this way of thinking in the future.

## The Aim of This Book

It is important to remember that palmistry as a science can be exceptionally detailed. The aim of this book is to familiarise you with the rudiments of the subject, and perhaps stimulate you and lead you on to further study.

Palmistry is not difficult to master and can be great fun. You can learn a lot about yourself and others, and maybe surprise your friends by your insight into their character and past, which will set their minds wondering how you could possibly know so much. Is it magic? No, it's palmistry!

# CHAPTER 1 – Looking At Hands

The only time many people look at their hands is when they are washing them, cutting their nails, or putting on rings, hand cream or nail varnish. However, hands are fascinating and deserve to be studied more closely! Hands are more than tools for picking up objects. Men in particular seldom really look at either their own hands or those of others. I would like to see more men interested in palmistry. They may well be surprised at what they learn about themselves, not Just other people!

I have always felt that everyone should learn as much about themselves as possible, and this includes learning about their own hands. Many people will visit a palmist at some point during their lives. Sometimes, it is to learn more about themselves, sometimes it is a desire to know about the future, sometimes it is just curiosity, and sometimes they need genuine advice. Someone who is trained in palmistry can, indeed, tell at a glance where your true talents lie, where health problems exist or are likely to exist, how you can avoid the pitfalls of ill-health, and how best for you to proceed in certain circumstances. It is all there, written in your own hands, and the hands of everyone around you, but you are unable to see it for yourself. However, with a little help from this book you should be able to look at hands objectively, and learn from what you see.

It is not a question of being psychic or intuitive in any way; all the answers are there for you to see. Many palmists may also be psychic, and some psychic palmists merely use the vibrations they pick up from holding the hand, and don't actually read the palm itself at all. It is, however, not necessary for the amateur palmist to be psychic to start to learn about palmistry

# Getting started

One of the essential tools of the trade for someone who wants to be a palmist is a large, reliable magnifying glass, preferably one with a handle so that you can look at the lines and trends on the hand with ease. However, if you just want to learn palmistry for fun, see how you get on before deciding to invest in one. (Many people have magnifying glasses in their houses already and anything larger than two inches in diameter will do the job.) Serious palmists often have equipment to take hand prints, but this is only really necessary for professionals.

Just start by looking at your own hands. What do they feel like? Are they rough, smooth, flexible? What colour are they? Are they red, white, pink? What are your nails like? Are your fingers square- or round-ended? Are your hands hot, cold, warm, moist? All these aspects, and more, need to be considered before even starting to look at the lines and mounts. So this is where we shall begin.

## The Basic Shapes

As we have already established, palmistry is not just the study of the lines of the hand; you must take into account the whole hand, and that includes the shape of the hand.

What shape is your hand? Hand shape gives you the basic information on personality and character, and is the foundation for further work. You should look at the basic shape of the hand before even starting to look at the nails, skin, palm, etc. It is easy to look at the shape of people's hands without them being aware of it, and you may decide to begin to do this as a matter of course to see how many different hand-types you can spot.

Below you will see seven hand-types. Which hand-type is yours? Look carefully before going any further, as it is important to realise which category you personally fall into, before looking at others.

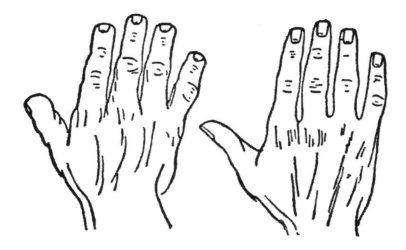

Left : The Elementary Hand
Right: The Square Hand

## The Square Hand

This is probably the commonest type of hand, and relatively easy to spot and to work on. Sometimes the fingers won't match the hand shown here, exactly; some square-handed people will have longer fingers than others and obviously this is something which you need to consider. Square-handed people with short fingers are likely to be narrower minded than a square-handed person with longer fingers, but whether long or short fingered, these people are methodical, open people, normally hardworking and pillars of the community. They may never get to the top of their profession, but will keep battling on, providing they see a reason for doing so. This hand is often found on carpenters, mechanics, architects and inventors. Generally disliking change of any kind, they are never fanatical about anything, whether it be politics, religion or viewpoint. They have a respect for authority and like anything logical or methodical. People with these hands often have problems showing their true feelings and dislike anything rash or impetuous. They make honest, dependable spouses but may not be very romantic or exciting. For this reason they get on best with other square-handed people. Square-handed people are often found amongst Northern Europeans.

## The Elementary Hand

A hand that looks as if it belongs to Early Man. It is not a pretty hand; the fingers are short and stubby, whilst the palm can be many differing shapes, but is normally thick. The hands look clumsy and coarse, and often there will be few lines on the palm. People from the Arctic regions or northern parts of Russia often have these hands: people who chop trees, work hard and live a hard instinctive life. They do not usually have an appreciation of beauty but they are often good with animals, plants and the world of nature, something which is of great importance to them. These people are not generally intellectual, seem to act from instinct rather than reason, and be totally without emotion or aspirations. This hand, often regarded as the lowest type of hand, is seldom seen in women, and rarely in its pure form.

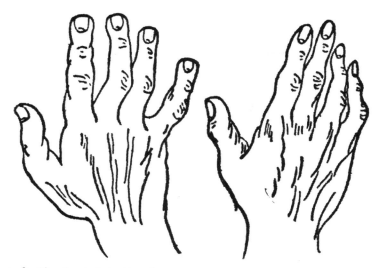

Left: The Spatulate Hand
Right: The Philosophic Hand

## The Philosophic Hand

Knotted fingers are the main sign of the Philosophic Hand. The
palm is normally rectangular, the fingers bony and the joints
large. These people are methodical thinkers and seldom
become wealthy. People with this type of hand fall into two
categories - materialists or idealists. They tend to be students
and explorers in the intellectual sense, wanting to know about
religion, politics and the inner spirituality of being. They have an
interest in mankind but are very private people, reserved, silent,
proud, secretive, and somewhat outside the natural group. They
prefer to view a group from outside rather than from within.
But they will be observing closely, and if asked for an opinion
will give wise advice. Hard workers and honest, both with
others and with themselves, they will endure hardships without
complaining. They have few real friends, and are a poor match
with the conic hand-type. This type of hand is relatively
common in India and the Orient, and amongst mystics of all

nationalities. It is interesting to note how many people belonging to the earth signs (Capricorn, Virgo and Taurus) have this sort of hand, as do Aquarians. It is also interesting how many people working in the New Age sector have the Philosophic Hand.

## The Spatulate or Active Hand

A large, wide hand, with thick, sometimes long, fingers with broad tips. These people are the active members of the community, people who are original and restless by nature and prefer to act rather than think. They love any form of gamble, risk or speculation. They will keep going until they drop and are often linked with explorers or the early settlers in America, those pioneers who battled their way across the plains in search of a new home. A love of action, independence and energy means these people will not be held back or restricted in any way. For this reason, they often have a  disrespect of law and authority. They are originals, and it is often thought that women with this hand-type are psychic. They are people who are naturally athletic and sometimes musical also. This sort of hand can be found amongst all types of people in all sorts of professions. They are all intent on making a mark in life and are true individuals, making their own rules and regulations as they go along. It is probable that many of the people around you have this hand-type. Indeed, your own hand may fall into this category. Take a look and see!

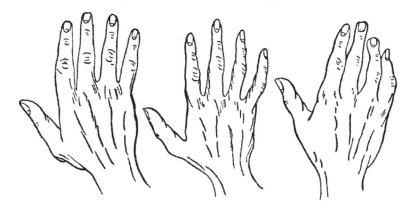

Left: Conic Hand
Middle: The Psychic Hand
Right: The Mixed Hand

## The Conic Hand

The owners of this hand, sometimes also known as the Temperamental Hand, are usually artistic, poetic, gifted and imaginative. The hands are medium sized with attractive, tapering fingers, and the palm is quite slender. These people are the charmers of this world. Idealistic, sensitive and volatile, they dislike the mundane and have a vivid imagination and unusual desires. They often act purely on impulse, and lack patience and business sense. They are good conversationalists, often knowing a little about a lot of different subjects. They are people with many acquaintances but few they consider to be true, or close friends. Easily influenced by others, they are plain-speakers and sometimes quick-tempered. They appreciate beauty in their surroundings, are usually bad at managing money, and prefer writing, painting, or composing to any physical activity. Many people with this type of hand are gifted musicians or artists. They are always in search of new pursuits and need to have personal freedom to be at their best. Love is fundamental to their being, and they tend to be emotional, impulsive and excitable. Many people with the Conic Hand are charity workers. People with this type of hand seem to get on with everyone, and are often from a Greek, Italian or Spanish background.

## The Psychic Hand

These are delicate hands, slim with pointed fingers and narrow palms. A pure Psychic Hand is not common. These people see beauty in everything, and are the world's idealists. For this reason, many palmists refer to the Psychic Hand as the Pointed or Idealistic Hand. These people need love but often choose the wrong partner. Finding it difficult to cope with traumas and set-backs, they need someone to look after them and are often very sensitive and vulnerable. They are normally very impractical and have no sense of time and will frequently be found with their head in a book of poetry. They tend to be illogical, have poor business sense, are easily influenced and imposed upon by others, and as a result, often become depressed. They are ruled by the heart and highly strung. Don't fall into the trap of looking at a woman's hand and automatically classifying it as Psychic or Conic. Look at it more carefully. To be a true Psychic Hand there should also be a Psychic Cross on the Fate Line, but we will discuss this later.

## The Mixed Hand

This is the hand that does not fit into any of the above categories and contains elements of most of the different types of hand. The palm may be large and the fingers long, but it may also show characteristics of the Elementary Hand or the Conic Hand. The way to look at these hands is to look for the most important features and go from there. These people are individuals, adaptable and difficult to categorise. They may be able to tackle a wide variety of jobs, and do them all with a reasonable degree of success. They are often restless people, who like to move locations a great deal. People with the Mixed Hand are sometimes engineers or inventors. Now we can recognise the different types of hand, all from looking at the back of the hand without even looking at the palm, let's look at some other important factors. (Women's hands are normally smaller than the male hand, and the features may not be as strong, but they will still be visible.)

## Sizes of Hand

One of the first things to look at is the size of the hand in comparison to the size of the body. In very general terms, people with small hands are ambitious achievers, often thinking unrealistically and aiming too high. They almost always have large, bold handwriting. People with big hands, however, are people who are easily contented and have an interest in and are good at working with detail, and normally have small writing.

Looking at the type of palm, we can generalise that a thin palm is likely to show a nervous person, a thick palm a somewhat egotistical and passionate person, a firm, yet malleable, palm a quick-thinking person, and a soft palm a person who loves luxury. Again, in general terms, a narrow palm shows someone who is conventional and often miserable or unhappy, a hollow palm someone who lacks direction and aggression, and is likely to suffer a lot of mishaps and disappointments during their lifetime.

## Colour and Skin Texture

Look to see what colour the hand is - does it look like the hand of someone who works outside or someone who always has their hands in water? What is the texture of the skin? Generally, fine, smooth skin belongs with sensitive, delicate people who are calm and even-tempered, whereas rougher skin indicates those who are hard working, active and vigorous. Most people, however, come somewhere between these extremes.

If the hands are white, they are likely to show a selfish and uncaring person, while red hands indicate someone who is warm and caring.

A yellow skin (unless on a person of Oriental background) shows someone who is changeable, whereas a darker skin colour (not related to Ethnic background) shows someone who is well-balanced and fair-minded.
Hairy hands are said to show inconsistency, whereas hairless hands show cowardice.
People with soft hands are often nervous and impressionable, whereas people with harder hands are likely to be practical and solid.

## Skin Patterns

The study of the skin patterns on the hands, and on the fingers in particular, is very detailed, and could occupy a book on its own. However, for our purposes, and before going on to look at the lines on the hand in detail, a cursory look at the skin will show that the pattern is either open or closed. By this I mean that a closed pattern will show lots of small lines and an open pattern will show wide lines with more spaces. An open skin pattern indicates a person who is open and active, and unrefined, especially when the hand is soft, whereas a closed skin pattern shows someone who is gentle and lethargic, especially when the hand is soft.

When looking at skin patterns, professional palmists will look at fingerprints, and in particular at loops, whorls, arches and tented arches and composites. When looking at the palm, they will study palmar loops. However, as we have already discussed, this is very detailed work, and is best studied at a time after the basics of palmistry have been mastered and practised.

## Personality Types

What is the hand like? What is the handshake like? A soft handshake normally belongs to a lethargic sort of person, but this is a generality and you must look to the lines of the hand for more definite information. It is very easy to generalise on character-types from these features, but it would be very wrong to discount these characteristics, just because they are generalisations.

## Health from the Hands

The health of a person is immediately visible from looking at the hand, and in the last few years the medical profession worldwide has acknowledged this to some degree. There are many nerves in the hands and the palm of the hand can indicate positive or negative nerve conditions. The colour of the palm is most important. When pale, the person is likely to be selfish and unsympathetic; when pink, however, the person is likely to be hopeful and healthy. A red palm indicates a robust constitution, a yellow palm someone who suffers from depression and melancholy.

The colour of the hands shows vitality as well as health. Pink handed people are more energetic than red-handed people. White handed people are ultra-calm and often also pessimistic. Yellow hands in Europeans show problems with the liver, and these people are often highly-strung and nervous.

It is important to look at the temperature of the hands to get an overall picture of the health of the person concerned. Hands that are always hot and sweaty may indicate a thyroid or gland problem; hot, dry hands may indicate a blood problem. Cold, dry hands and hands that are cold in places show problems with circulation.  Hands that feel sticky are likely to indicate a liver problem.

## The Nails

Many doctors can look at a person's nails and see signs indicating health problems. (For instance white flecks in the nails show that zinc is missing from the diet.) Like white flecks, however, some of these signs are not permanent, and this is something you should always bear in mind when looking for health indications in the hands. Remember that discussing health is a difficult issue. Try where possible to give general advice rather than what may look like a diagnosis. Unless you are medically qualified, this can be dangerous.

The nails can reveal a lot about people, apart from health problems. Anybody can immediately notice when a person doesn't look after their nails or has dirty nails, and these observations, together with their overall appearance, form an impression as to the character of the person. People who bite their nails will be immediately considered to be nervous people; people with perfect nails, however, will be seen as people who take pride in themselves and their appearance.

The natural colour of the nails also should be taken into account. People who have white nails are generally unhappy, calm yet cold people. Pink nails indicate balance and a sympathetic nature, red show anger and passion, and dark nails or nails with a purple hue indicate someone is suffering from circulatory problems, or temporary ill health. Those with white specks on their nails are often bothered by nervous problems, and, as already stated, a lack of zinc in their diet.

Before making any comments on the health of the person concerned, be sure to look at the Health Line and other health indications on the hand. Ridges across the nail can indicate illness, or the fact that someone has been ill and is now recovering but is still affected by nervousness. Ridges running from top to bottom can often show someone with back or spinal problems. Again, think about what to say before making firm statements on this. Health is a very delicate issue, and it is easy to do more harm than good by being rash in giving health indications.

The shape of the nail can also give indications on personality. Square nails show balance, small, square nails stubbornness, round nails quick-temper, and almond nails an artistic temperament. Bent nails which resemble claws show people who are always on the go and long, filbert nails show balance. These are again, generalisations, and the whole hand, together with the lines must be looked at before making judgements on personality type.

## Family Traits

You should always check both hands, placing them side by side. There will almost certainly be differences between them, and even a casual look can often reveal marked differences. Should this be the case, and the hands seem quite different from each other, the person is likely to have had a very interesting and eventful life.

By tradition, your potential from birth and inherited family traits, plans, feelings and wishes are shown in your left hand and your right hand is your adult self. What is seen in your right hand is normally what you have done with your life. what you have experienced and accomplished (or not), and what you have made of your inherited traits.

If looking for answers to the future, always look at the left hand on a right-handed person. However, if they are left-handed, this should be reversed, and if they are ambidextrous, whilst not reversed, it may be that the tendencies will be muted - the left hand will still relate to the past, but the right will relate more to the present and future.

Practice will show that left-handed people often have the lines more clearly marked on their left hand, whereas the opposite is true for right-handed people.

## Fingers and Finger Lengths

Looking at the fingers tells you about the mind of a person, as the fingers represent the mind, and the remainder of the hand material aspects.
Discounting the palm, it is easy to spot long and short fingers. Long fingered people are analytical, lovers of detail and are normally well dressed, quick-thinking and of a nervous temperament, inclined to worry and restlessness. Short-fingered people are normally quick, impulsive and rash. They are not interested in their appearance, dislike detail, authority and tradition and are naturally rebellious. Should the fingers be short and thick, the person is likely to be .selfish.

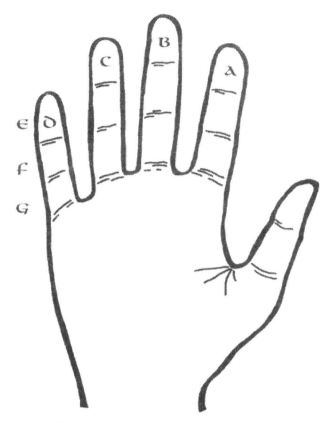

A – Jupiter Finger
B – Saturn Finger
C – Sun Finger
D – Mercury Finger
E – First Phlange
F – Second Phlange
G – Third Phlange

In most people, the second finger, or Saturn Finger, is the longest, the third, the ring or Sun Finger (also sometimes called the Apollo Finger) is next in size, then the index or Jupiter Finger, and finally the little finger or Mercury Finger is the shortest. Normally, the index finger will be about 80 per cent of the length of the second or Saturn Finger, and the Sun (or third) Finger will be about 90 per cent of the Saturn Finger. The little or Mercury Finger is usually 70 per cent of the Saturn Finger.

When the index finger is very long, the person concerned is likely to be rather domineering and dictatorial. Should the finger be as long as the Saturn (second) Finger, the desire for power will be more marked. When the Sun Finger is nearly the same length as the Jupiter Finger there is ambition for money and its trappings. A gambler is likely to have an extremely long Sun Finger, longer than the others. They will gamble with money and life and possibly also have artistic talents. A long Mercury (little) Finger shows someone who communicates well, is a talented writer and something of a philosopher.

Should you, or someone you know, have fingers which are so supple that they can be bent back, this indicates a charming person who is good company, pleasant and intelligent, but also naturally inquisitive. People with stiff fingers are likely to be reserved, cautious and lacking in the spirit of adventure.

Someone with fingers which are thick at the base is likely to consider his own comforts before those of anyone else and be fond of eating and drinking; narrow-based fingers show someone who is totally the opposite.


## Thumbs

The thumb is obviously important in its own right and represents will-power and energy levels. Many palmists will say that one look at the thumb will give a very good indication of character, as the thumb shows the person as an individual.

Look at the thumb and how it lies against the fingers. Again, as with fists and general hand positions, a thumb which lies close to the fingers means someone who is not very generous and is an introverted person. A looser thumb indicates a more free-thinking person; if the thumb is stiff and unbending, this shows someone who is reserved, obstinate even, with strong views which are often aired. With thumbs, you should always look for flexibility, as this gives an insight into the flexibility of its owner. Obviously, if someone is standing with their hands stiff, they are also likely to be intolerant or stiff; relaxed hands show relaxed people. Someone with a broad or naturally flattened thumb is said to be passionate and hot-blooded. Long thumbs are thought to indicate intellectual willpower; short thumbs show lethargy, obstinacy, unreliability and a weak will.

When looking at thumbs, break them down into phalanges, or sections. The thumb has only two phalanges. The first, or top, section is associated with will-power and intellectual capacity; the second with logic and reasoning powers. The base of the thumb is associated with love, and some palmists suggest that there is a third phalange where the thumb and palm meet against the boundary of the Mount of Venus but this is for more advanced study only.

When the first phalange is long, the person has strong reasoning powers, and yet will be affected by the opinions of other people, especially if the point of the thumb seems long and tapering. Should the first phalange seem thick, it shows a domineering person who is obstinate and aggressive, but a good leader. Should, however, the first phalange be thin, the person is likely to be a calmer individual, good with people and possess great charm. A short first phalange indicates a weak-willed person. To look at the second phalange, you must compare its length with the first. When the second phalange is long, there is a lack of will-power and determination, although the person is likely to be just and fair, and analytical. A short second phalange reflects the intuitive type of person, whereas first and second phalanges of similar length show a logical and well-balanced person. When the third phalange is long and the thumb small, it indicates a passionate person. More information on this area of the thumb and the Mount of Venus will be given later.

As we have already seen, it is important when looking at the thumb to take into account whether the thumb is flexible or stiff.

The supple thumb, normally seen in Italians, Spanish, French and Irish peoples, indicates a person who is extravagant with money and time. These people are friendly and adaptable, broad-minded and generous. The firm-jointed thumb, however, indicates an inbuilt caution and obstinacy, with narrow-minded views and a stubbornness of character. These people are far more practical than the supple thumb type. Secrecy, lack of emotion and a keen sense of justice are often their main characteristics.

## The Palm

It is important to look at the length of the palm. The palm is normally shorter in length than the fingers, but if this is not the case, this shows someone who is practical rather than intellectual.

# The Jupiter Finger

As mentioned earlier, the fingers are named after the planets. The first finger, index finger or Jupiter Finger signifies your ego, or self. It denotes confidence, reliability.

Short index fingers tend to show people who dislike any form of responsibility, whilst a long index finger will show a person who is capable and has leadership potential. If it leans towards the thumb, this shows an ambitious and independent nature. If, however, the tip of the finger leans towards the middle, this shows that actions are thought through and nothing is done on the spur of the moment. Should the Jupiter Finger be shorter than the Sun (or ring) Finger, this is someone who is a good leader, someone who knows what they want and may not worry about how they get it.

As with the thumb, professional palmists divide fingers into sections, or phalanges, and you can get even more information from these. A long top phalange shows a well-developed intellect; a short top phalange shows a tendency towards practicality and the need for security. A long middle phalange shows an orderly person; a short middle phalange shows a person lacking in direction and ambition. A long third or bottom phalange shows a sporty person; a short third phalange shows a sensible person.

# The Saturn Finger

The middle or Saturn Finger is your attitude finger, how you view life.

Sometimes an indication of seriousness, a long middle finger belongs to a person with firm ideas, a stubborn, moody, cautious person who prefers to work alone and takes life seriously; a short Saturn Finger is the person who takes nothing seriously, is often rash and impetuous, and may enjoy creating havoc. If the Saturn Finger leans towards the ring finger, it can show a passive person who needs material and emotional security; if the finger leans away from the ring finger, the person prefers their own company.

A long top phalange shows someone who is naturally inquisitive and interested in details. A short top phalange shows an easy-going person who is likely to be easily dominated. A long middle phalange shows a mathematical bias; a short middle phalange shows a person who is extravagant. A long third phalange shows someone who is unreliable and materialistic; a short third phalange shows a person who is likely to watch their bank balance carefully.

## The Sun Finger

The Sun (ring) Finger, if 'normal' length, shows someone who is artistic and good in business. It is the finger showing creativity, style and talents.

A person whose Sun Finger is the same length as the middle finger is usually someone who doesn't mind taking risks to achieve their goals. The longer the Sun Finger, the more of a gambler the person is likely to be, whether this be someone who gambles on horses or dogs, or someone who gambles in a speculative sense on the Stock Market or in a job situation. These people seldom think things through, and can often come unstuck as a result. A short Sun Finger will show someone lacking in enthusiasm, especially for gambling, someone who isn't normally good in the business world, being overcautious by nature. These people are not usually artistic in any way. Someone whose Sun Finger displays a rounded top could be an actor or have dramatic flair. If the finger is also long, they will be creative and artistic people, possibly interested in the theatre, drama or films.

A long top phalange shows someone who is dramatic and creative; a short top phalange shows someone who is not interested in art at all. A long second phalange shows someone who is good with design and colour; a short second phalange reveals the opposite. A long third phalange shows refined taste and an interest in objects of art; a short third phalange reveals someone who may be extremely lacking in artistic talent.

## The Mercury Finger

The Mercury (little) Finger is the communication finger. You can tell from this whether someone is a talker or not.

A normal-size Mercury Finger belongs to someone who is tactful, capable, sensitive and kind, especially if the finger also leans towards the Sun (ring) Finger. (Discount any leanings of the finger due to the jewellery or rings. In fact it is best to ask people to take any jewellery off, as a bulky ring will throw the fingers next to it out of alignment.) A Mercury Finger which seems to lean away from the other fingers suggests a person who will never become one of the crowd. A short Mercury Finger will show someone who is supercritical of all around and a lack of confidence. A person with a long Mercury Finger, however, is usually the centre of any gathering, exuding charm and with the ability to talk on most subjects, and sometimes also speak several languages. These people are normally leaders in their field.

A long top phalange shows someone who misses nothing, is charming and well-read; a short top phalange shows a person who is reserved and shy. A long middle phalange shows a person who is likely to be interested in health and diet; a short middle phalange shows a person who is faithful and steadfast. A long third phalange shows someone who is well-spoken and needs their own space; a short third phalange shows a person who is impressionable and easily duped.

## Looking at Yourself

Have you looked at your own hand, and seen into which categories you can place yourself? Have you been subjective about this? Maybe it would be a good idea to ask someone else to check your interpretations, as they may look at things a little differently.

It is easy to see only your good points and not so easy to see the points which need to be worked upon. The thing to remember at all times, not only with palmistry but with anything which lays bare your character, is to see things which may seem negative as chances to become better and improve. Such bad points are not criticisms but serve to focus the attention and allow room for personal growth. If your friends are helping you with this subjective viewing be sure to take what they say in good part, trying not to view their agreement to any negativity as criticisms. If you see, for example, that your hand reveals you to be stubborn or moody, should you just take this as part and parcel of your character or should you decide this is a part of you with which you are not happy, and try to do something about it? In this way palmistry can truly help your personal growth.

Practice

At the end of every chapter, we will have a small question section. No answers will be given, and the idea is to help you to think back over the chapter before progressing. Don't panic – the questions are fairly easy.

• How many hand types have we discussed? Name these.

- Would you expect to see many people with the Elementary Hand?
- What is the name given to the middle finger?
- What is a phalange?
- What information, in general terms, is shown in the left hand, on the assumption that we are talking about a right-handed person?
- Are the fingers named after planets or places on earth?

## CHAPTER 2 – The Major Lines

There are seven important lines on the hand, but three main ones: the Life Line, the Head Line and the Heart line.

The Life Line, sometimes also called the Vital Line, is a gentle curve round the fleshy base of the thumb (known to palmists as the Mount of Venus). The Head Line crosses the centre of the hand and the Heart Line runs parallel to the Head Line at the base of the fingers.

The Life Line relates to the life of the person, the length of life and the major changes in the lifetime. On the Life Line we can find time spans, illnesses and important events.

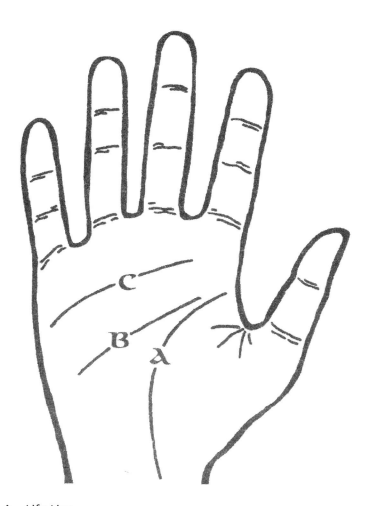

A – Life Line
B – Head Line
C – Heart Line
The Head Line shows intellectual strengths and weaknesses, the temperament and what use is being made of any talents.
The Heart Line, sometimes called the Mensa', shows love, attraction and the emotional events in the lifetime of the person.

Below, is a diagram showing other four important lines, which we will discuss later.

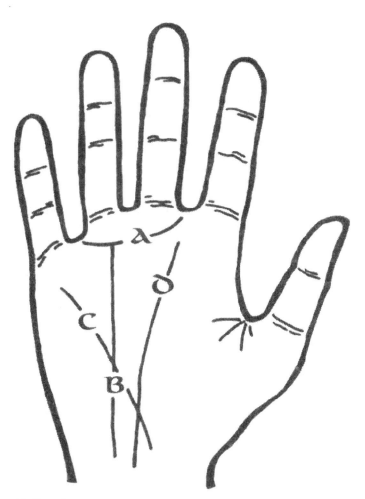

A – Girdle of Venus
B – Sun Line
C – Health Line
D – Fate Line

# The Life Line

As you will see from the illustration, the Life Line runs round the Mount of Venus. There may be a continuous line, or there may be gaps in the line. It may end near the wrist, or in a number of different places. The line may move into the palm, fork once or twice or just fade away. Should the latter be the case, please don't become concerned with the length of the Life Line, trying to establish from it the length of the life. Anybody who engages in this form of prediction or speculation can cause unnecessary worry, concern and, ultimately, damage.

There are so many things which can be learnt from the Life Line without resorting to concerns of death. The Life Line shows a person's approach to life, their energy levels and constitution. It should be recognised from the outset that a short Life Line does not necessarily indicate a short life, nor a long Life Line indicate a long one. This traditional interpretation, begun centuries ago, is far from reliable. To look for life indications, you should look for a well formed line with a dark-pink colour, showing a strong, robust constitution. The line should be deep, long and well-marked, without any breaks or interruptions, and sweep out into the palm to show good vitality and constitution, and an extrovert and spontaneous nature. If it appears to be the strongest of the three main lines, it can be assumed that physical concerns are paramount to that person, and that they probably work outdoors or at least prefer to be outdoors.

## Looking at Both Hands

It is always best to look at both hands and compare Life Lines. Should the Life Line on the left hand not go into the palm as much as the Life Line on the right hand, this shows a person who has made a determined effort towards individuality and has worked hard to get on in life. Breaks in the Life Line also need to be followed through by looking at the other hand.

Breaks in this line are generally indications of illnesses, and a look at the other hand should show whether these are serious or not. When the Life Line is broken in the left hand and continuous in the right hand, there is likely to have been a serious illness, or an illness of this nature is to come, depending upon where on the Life Line the break occurs. Any sort of mark, chaining, break etc., shows poor health. Should the Life Line start under the Jupiter Finger and be chained (Le look like small circles all joined together), this is an indication of ill-health in childhood.

## Looking at Career

We can learn about the career of the person concerned from looking at the Life Line. Career-minded people, as a general rule, have Life Lines which seem to go well into the centre of the hand. This also indicates good physical strength and a long life. Should the line, however, stay close to the Mount of Venus, the person is likely to suffer from poor health. Sometimes, the line will seem to stop and then start again, reaching into the centre of the hand. This would indicate someone whose career became important later in life, such as a woman who had taken up a career after the children had grown up. Should the Life Line start at the base of the Jupiter Finger at what is known as the Mount of Jupiter, instead of at the side of the hand, this indicates an ambitious person; should it start lower down, the person may be less ambitious. A fork at the end of the Life Line, indicates someone who wants to travel.

## Timings

There are two schools of thought on timing events using the lines on the hand. One of the oldest was used by the travelling gypsies, who took a pair of compasses and put the point to the exact centre of the base of the Jupiter Finger, and the other end to the centre of the base of the Saturn Finger. Allowing the compass to swing towards the Life Line, the point where it crossed was said to represent the 10th year of life. Keeping the pointer still, and extending the compass to the base of the Sun Finger, then swinging it down to the Life Line marked the 30th year of life, and so on. This method does not always work, due to variable line formations, and other palmists have worked out timings by dividing the life line into 15 sections, each of 5 years in length. This is obviously an approximation but is sufficient to put events into some kind of a time-scale. People live to Widely differing ages, and we must not presume that the standard length of a life is 75 years, just by making these divisions.


Working out timings from the Life Line

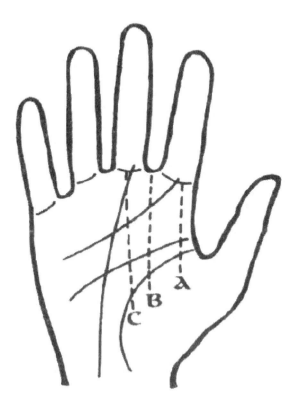

A = 10 years     B = 20 years     C = 35 years

## Other Features

There are times when people have on their life lines marks which themselves indicate certain things. These marks, called crosses, forks, grilles, squares etc. are separate items, and will be dealt with later. At present it is only necessary to look at the major lines.

Here are a few illustrations of Life Lines which do not follow the standard pattern.

Life Line with chaining at the beginning, showing early problems or unhappiness, possibly health-related, or some form of restriction.

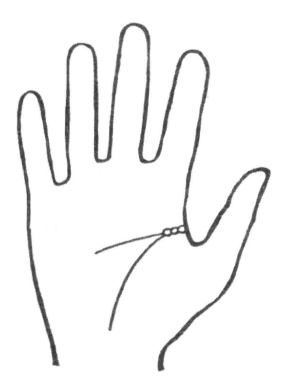

Life Line which fades and then reappears, showing a health problem.

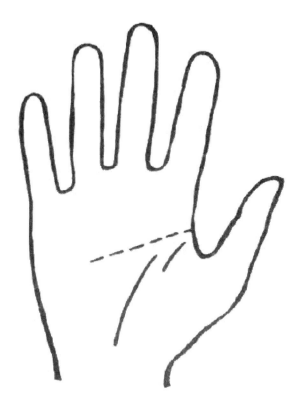

What looks like a double Life Line, but is in effect the inner Life Line or Line of Mars, adding strength to the Life Line.

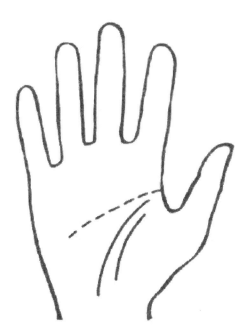

The short Life Line, which breaks then, reappears in a stronger form. This shows someone who has started again, probably after a set-back. This is often seen in people who have begun a new life in new circumstances.

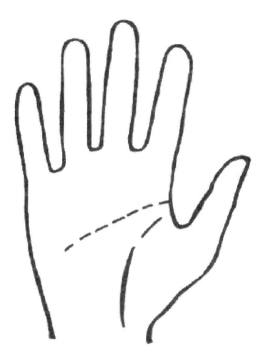

The Life Line which seems to be straight, showing inhibition and lethargy.

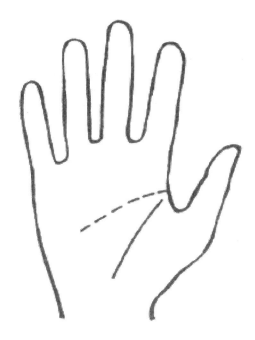

## The Head Line

The Head Line relates to mental ability, potential, and level of perception. Should the Head Line be missing altogether or appear very faint, this shows someone who is unable to concentrate for long periods of time.

Ideally, the Head Line should start very near to the Life Line, and extend into the palm to finish just below the middle of the Mercury (little) Finger. This would indicate someone with strong intellect, independence and realism. If, however, the Head Line starts from inside the Life Line, the person is likely to be inhibited, a born worrier, inconsistent, highly-strung, insecure and lacking in confidence. A Head Line which seems joined to the start of the Life Line shows a cautious individual, someone inhibited, conventional, nervous, sensitive, and possibly tied to the family. If the Head Line, however, seems to start high up near the Mount of Jupiter, the person will be balanced, honest, logical and intellectual, with good leadership and organisational qualities. A Head Line which starts from the Mount of Jupiter and just touches the Life Line is likely to belong to a powerful person who is talented, ambitious and strong.

This is especially so if the line is long. Should the Head Line appear short, the person concerned will probably be down-to-earth and practical, possessing a retentive memory, but little imagination. If the line fails to reach the middle of the hand, the person will be practical and materialistic. A long Head Line, however, which seems to slope dramatically, shows someone who has too many interests (probably of a creative nature), and lacks concentration but has a good imagination. This person is likely to be interested in music, literature and the arts. The degree of slope indicates the amount of interest. Very straight Head Lines show obstinate, selfish, rather aloof yet highly intelligent personalities, especially if the line seems to go to the outside of the hand.

The head will rule the heart should the Head Line be very near the Line of the Heart, whereas when there is a reasonable, but not large, space between the Head Line and the Life Line, the person will be confident and helpful. A large space between these two lines indicates a rash, impatient personality.

## Looking at Both Hands

Again, it is necessary to compare the Head Lines in both hands, as the right hand will show what the person has made of inherited traits. A strong line in the right hand indicates someone who has been able to follow their own desires and been successful; a weak line in the right hand will show someone who is less determined. Should both Head Lines in the hands appear similar, this is a person who has accepted and made the best of situations. Should the line in the right hand fade and then seem to reappear, this may show someone who has had problems keeping going at times, and again reference to the left hand will show whether this has been a family trait. A Head Line which is broken in two on both hands can indicate an accident to the head.

## Timings

It is not easy to time events using the Head Line. In general terms, however, the first half of the line, from just under the Jupiter Finger towards the outer edge relates to the 35-40 age range, whereas the second half of the line relates to 40-70 or 75.

## Other Features

Here are a few diagrams showing various Head Lines which you may come across.

A Head Line which ends in a fork showing creativity, possibly writing, or someone who has two careers at one time.

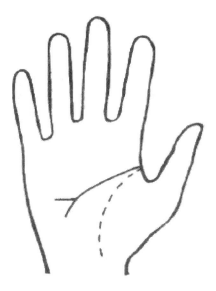

A Head Line which cuts across the palm, showing will-power, ambition and a lack of emotion.

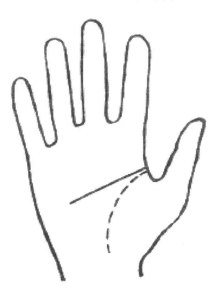

A double Head Line showing someone who is idealistic to the extreme, has two differing lifestyles or careers, and unusual talents.

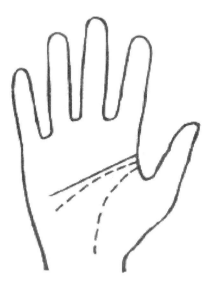

A chained Head Line showing lack of concentration and logic, probably due to health difficulties or stress.

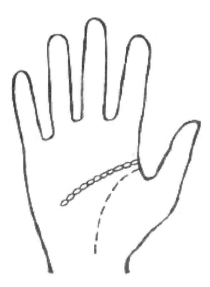

A branched Head Line, showing interruptions to ambitions and setbacks.

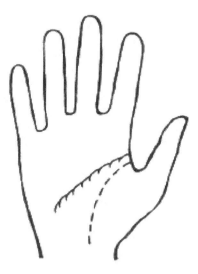

# The Heart Line

The line of the Heart reveals, as would seem obvious from its name, everything to do with love and attraction, moods and emotions, sensitivities and some health matters. To those people that have an interest in potential relationships, this is the line to look towards, as it indicates the type of relationships which have occurred in the past and are likely to be formed in the future.

The classic Heart Line should start between the Jupiter and Saturn Fingers, and curve to end below the Mercury Mount at the edge of the palm. It should be clear and well-marked and, when in the ideal position, shows a well-adjusted person with a warm, deep, sentimental, caring and outgoing personality. The influence of Jupiter in general makes for a passionate individual, yet one who needs understanding; the deeper the line, the more sensual the person tends to be. When the line seems to start more towards Saturn, the person is likely to be less ardent. Should the line be missing altogether, or seem to have faded, the person concerned is likely to be cold and indifferent, with very little feeling. When the line seems thin towards the outer part of the palm, the person may have relationship problems. Breaks in the Heart Line will show emotional setbacks or several love affairs.

There are various positions where the line may start and end. In general terms, should the line start high up on the hand, a convivial personality is indicated. When the line seems to drop down towards
the Head Line, the person is likely to have been unhappy during childhood or early adolescence and yet have benefited from the experience to grow as an individual. A Heart Line which seems to follow the Head Line, and appears to be joined to the Head Line shows a selfish personality, and it is best to see which of

the lines is more defined before making a judgement on the dominant characteristics.

The more the line seems to drop down into the palm, the more likely it is that the person concerned will be of a physical nature; the higher the line, the more likely is it that the person will be emotionally expressive. Little or no curve indicates little emotion. A Heart Line which starts from the centre of Jupiter shows a person who is reliable and trustworthy, whereas a Heart Line which starts from the Mount of Jupiter would indicate someone who is likely to put the target of his affections on an unrealistic pedestal, and be idealistic and very emotional.

It is not uncommon to find a person with forks either at the start or end of the Heart Line. Should the fork be at the start, with one branch seeming to rest on Jupiter and the other start between the Jupiter and Saturn Fingers, this is a happy person, well-adjusted and good company. Should the fork be wide and one fork actually be on Jupiter and the other on Saturn, the person is likely to be temperamental. If the line starts on Saturn and has a branch between the Mount of Saturn and Jupiter, the person is likely to be idealistic and intellectual. If the line forks at the end of the line on the Mercury Mount, the person is likely to be a charmer, a good communicator and friendly. A fork which seems to have three prongs is by tradition a lucky sign, with the person concerned being blessed with good fortune throughout life.

## Looking at Both Hands

As with the other main lines, it is important to compare both Heart Lines and look at both hands to note any differences. Should the differences be slight, the person is likely to be a happy individual, should the differences be marked, however, the likelihood is that the person will have many emotional ups and downs.

## Health

To show good health, it is traditional that the Heart Line be clear and well defined, with no breaks or variations. However, this is not always the case. Emotional problems can, and often do, result in health problems, whether mental or physical. Any chains, breaks or interruptions will therefore indicate an emotional problem which may have affected the person's health. By tradition, any such abnormality at the start of the Heart Line, especially if the line itself starts under the Mount of Saturn, indicates hearing problems. If the line starts from under the Mount of Apollo, there are likely to be eye problems. If there is a break or abnormality there, and if the abnormality is at the start and the line itself starts under the Mount of Mercury, the person may have blood pressure problems. These traditional meanings are generalisations, and it is probably wise to look at health indications in the rest of the hand before making any firm suggestions on health issues. Remember that health indications can be shown in the colour, texture and temperature of the hands and in the nails, as well as in the lines, and we shall learn about more features which give clues about health later in the book. Remember to look at all these sources before making any statements.

## Timings

There are various theories on how to judge time from the Heart Line, and these basically follow two main points of view - whether to judge from the inner or the outer side of the palm. Some people will in fact argue that it is impossible to time events using the Heart Line. In the East, the system is that you take a piece of string, run it along the length of the line and then fold it in half. The half-way mark is said to represent 35 years or thereabouts. This rule applies to all major lines. This system presumes that the average life-span is 70 years. This is, of course, not always the case and timings cannot, therefore, be precise

## Other Features

On the following pages are a few diagrams showing other types, of heart line which you may come across. However, these are by no means exhaustive.

A passionate person who may also be self-centred is shown when the Heart Line is very curved and starts on the Saturn Mount.

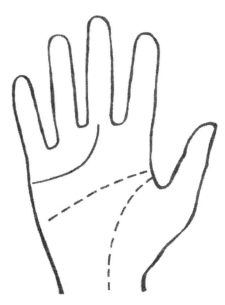

A chained Heart Line, or one which shows small breaks, indicates a person who is inconsistent, has contempt for others and may be a flirt.

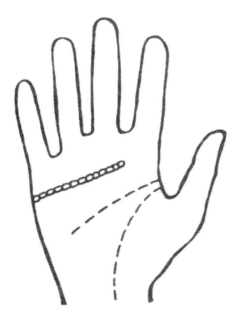

A short Heart Line shows lack of emotion and passion.

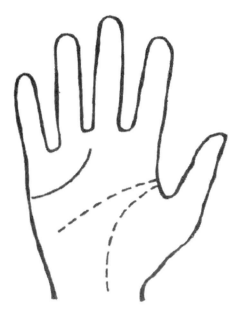

A romantic person with strong emotions is shown by a long Heart Line which seems to cut across the palm. The straighter the line the more emotion and companionship they may need.

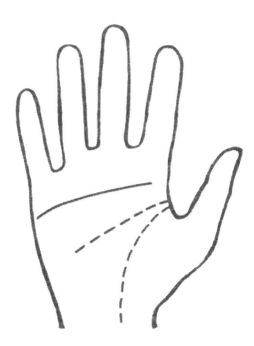

## Bracelets

Having looked at the three main lines on the hand, we are now going to take a brief look at the Bracelets around the wrist known as Rascettes or Wrist Rings. These are the lines at the base of the hand, where wrist joins palm.

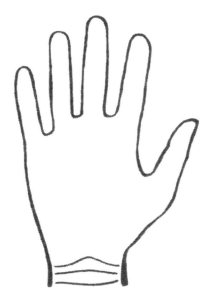

These have only minor importance in Western palmistry, but must be considered, as health indications can be shown by these lines. Students of Eastern palmistry may also look at the bracelets for signs of a long life, theorising that the more lines there are, the longer the person concerned will live.

Ideally, the Bracelets should cross the wrist in straight lines. Should the first Bracelet (the one nearest to the palm) be high on the wrist and rise towards the palm in an arch shape, there is every likelihood that the person may have an internal weakness of some kind, especially when the subject is a woman; there may be problems with the bladder or problems of a gynaecological nature, such as difficulty in having children. Should the second line also show arching, such difficulties are likely to be more pronounced. This is again somewhat of a generalisation, but is worth bearing in mind.

Traditionally, the more clearly defined the lines, the healthier the person; well-defined lines are likely to show someone who is unlikely to have even so much as travel sickness problems.

## Principles and Practice

During the course of this chapter, we have looked at the three lines most people will have heard about already, and hopefully learnt about some interesting features.

Taking a look at your own hand, have you learnt anything interesting about your own health, career, or emotions?

At this point it is important to stress that any health indications obtained from palmistry are indications only, and not hard-and-fast predictions. It is very important to take care when looking at health issues, as is the case when looking to answer questions on emotional matters or life expectancy. Should you be faced with a person, for example, with a short Life Line, it is vital that you put their mind at rest on the question of an early demise. Likewise, should problems of an emotional nature show up, bear in mind that different people will react to emotional setbacks in different ways. To one person they will be a major trauma, to another they may be something to be coped with and to grow from.

When looking at palms, and especially when dealing with other people, it is important that you remember your responsibilities, not only to yourself and your 'art' but to the other person. Try to be constructive; it is so very easy to be destructive, without intending to be. In my opinion, nobody should ever inform a person of a potentially life-threatening illness or death situation. This applies to reading cards, looking at palms, casting horoscopes or dealing with numerology. It is best, when faced with such situations, to refer someone to their own doctor or medical practitioner without frightening them. Merely suggesting regular health checks as a matter of course may resolve this predicament.

## Practice

At the end of this, the second chapter, we are going to be answering questions on the three main lines of the hand.

• Give the names of the three main lines.
• Does a short Life Line indicate a short life?
• We are looking at a palm where the Head Line and the Heart Line seem to run side by side. What would this indicate?
• What does a double Head Line show?
• We are looking at a palm where the Heart Line has a three pronged fork at its end. What would we conclude from this about the person's fortunes?
• Which line tells us about love, attraction and emotions?
• We are looking at a palm where the Life Line seems to stop half way and then restart. The person has just come to this country from abroad to live. Does this fit in?

# CHAPTER 3 – Other Important Lines

In this chapter we are going to look in a little more detail at the lines on the palm, and move on to cover four more important lines. These are the Fate Line, The Health Line, the Sun Line, and the Girdle of Venus. We will then have a look at a few other, smaller lines.

## The Fate Line

This is an important line to look for when asked to look for details of a person's career as it is also sometimes known by the name the Line of Destiny, Career Line or the Satumian Line. This is because it runs along the middle of the palm to the Mount of Saturn. (Should the line be present in this way, the person concerned is likely to be extremely successful, and feel in control of life, rather than feeling the victim of external factors.)

The Fate Line relates to anything material: to success, ambition, failure, career, other people's influences, and all external obstacles. It is said that people with a well-marked Fate Line are more likely to be responsible adults, with a sense of duty and discipline and have a steadier career than those whose Fate Line is less well-defined.

If you are looking at an elementary hand-type or square hand-type, you are likely to find the Fate Line less well-marked. It is said that the reason for this is because those with elementary or square hand types are less likely to believe in the power of fate than other hand types. This may be so, and it is interesting to see how often this is the case.

A true Fate Line will run from the wrist, up the palm, to the Saturn Finger. Sometimes it will be difficult to find, and often will be missing altogether. Those without a Fate Line are likely to be totally lacking ambition.

Some palmists maintain that a Fate Line which does not go from the wrist to the base of the Saturn Finger cannot be called a true Fate Line, but many times the Fate Line will not run the full length of the palm. In some instances, the Fate Line may actually reach into the Saturn Finger, rather than stopping at the base. If this is the case, there may be difficulties, and the power the person holds may not be easily controlled.

Again, it is important to look at both hands when looking at or for the Fate Line. From comparison, you can assess what a person has done with their inherited potential. It is rare that the Fate Lines in left and right hands will be the-same. Should the Fate Line appear in the left hand only, the person concerned is likely to be an idealist who falls short of fulfilling their 'ambitions; should the Fate Line appear in the right hand only, however, the person is likely to achieve their ambitions, provided they stay the course.

Should the Fate Line start from the Mount of Luna (the fleshy pad at the outer part of the hand near to the wrist), the person is likely to be independent, yet still dependent upon others to some degree. Should the line seem to be missing altogether and then appear from the Line of the Heart, success may come later in life. If the line seems to start from the Head Line, success may, again, come late in life, but the person's natural aptitude will see them through. A Fate Line which starts normally and then just stops is likely to indicate someone who gives up their career or whose ambitions stagnate.

If the Fate Line goes towards the Mount of Jupiter, rather than to the Saturn Finger, there is likely to be a great deal of success, more perhaps than if the line followed its traditional path. The person concerned is likely to put all their strength into their career. Jupiter brings determination to succeed.

A Fate Line which starts at the Life Line indicates a person who will have to work hard to succeed.

Sometimes the Fate Line will be forked, either at the start or end, and sometimes there will be several forks. If this is the case, and the forks are at the end of the line, it is particularly fortunate. If the fork is halfway through the line, which then starts again, the person is likely to have decided at that point to resign or change careers for a completely new start.

A broken Fate Line shows possible career changes throughout the person's lifetime. It is also common in people who are self-employed or who have to share their time between family commitments and their job. In general terms, if the break is from the Line of the Heart, the career change is less successful than anticipated, but again it is necessary to look at the whole hand for a full interpretation. If the new line seems to start closer to the thumb-side of the hand, the change is likely to have been beneficial; if it starts closer to the outer side of the hand the change may have come about because the person wanted to take up further study in order to secure better employment prospects. Should the Fate Line seem to have bars across it, there are likely to be barriers in the career progression.

On rare occasions, you may come across a double Fate Line. This indicates two careers, and to determine the ultimate outcome of these careers, it is necessary to see where they end.

It is sometimes possible to see from the Fate Line whether a person is likely to suffer from stress. Should the line end at Jupiter, take into account the overall health picture picked up from other sources. If the constitution is not particularly strong, such people are likely to suffer from stress, as their determination to succeed may not be matched by their general well-being. Look at the Heart Line in particular to see how emotions run, the Health Line, (which we will discuss shortly), as well as at the Life Line.

## Timings

Should the Fate Line end at the base of the Mount of Saturn and start near the wrist, the point at which it crosses the Head Line represents 30-35 years, or thereabouts, and where it passes over the Heart Line 40-45 years.

## Other Features

On the following pages are a few diagrams showing other features which may appear when looking at the Fate Line.

A Fate Line which seems to waver indicates a career which changes and is full of highs and lows.

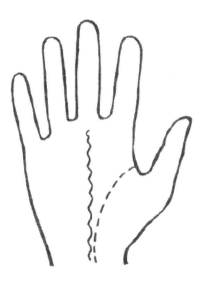

A Fate Line which stops at the Heart Line suggests that the career may be halted by a personal matter, the emotions or a relationship.

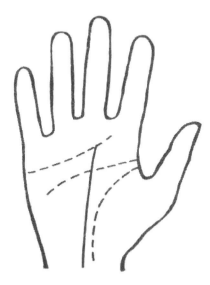

A Fate Line which stops at the Head Line suggests that the person may have career difficulties due to poor judgement.

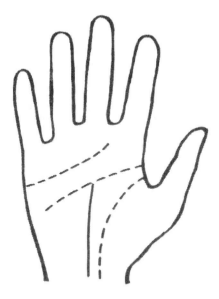

A Fate Line which cuts into and across the Life Line indicates other people will be material in the career of the person from an early age, probably to the person concerned's detriment. The person will probably be expected to follow family wishes.

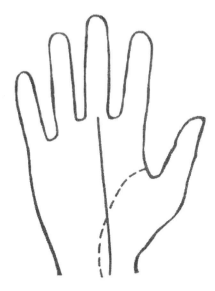

A Fate Line which ends at the Head Line and then reappears indicates a change of career; the second career undertaken will not be followed through with the passion of the first.

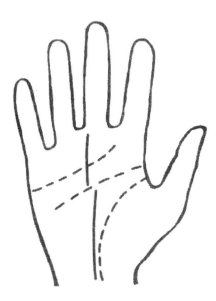

# The Health Line

Sometimes also known as the Hepatica, Liver or Mercury Line, the presence of this line indicates a preoccupation with health, ill-health, or both. People with this line in their palm are likely to be very sensitive, and often suffer with stomach or nervous problems or stress, especially when the line seems to be made up of segments. Some palmists maintain that it is more favourable, therefore, when this line is absent on a palm, and indeed, many men will be without a Health Line. The line can alter fairly regularly, and many palmists suggest that the line is a guide to health at that particular time, whereas the Life Line is the main guide to health and illness.

In most cases, the line lies straight down the hand, starting from on, or near, the Life Line, to end on the Mercury Mount, from which a good constitution to withstand health difficulties would be indicated. It is best for the line to keep well away from the Life Line. The well-defined Health Line suggests someone interested in health concerns, such as diet or lifestyle.

Some palmists suggest that it is possible to assess the sort of health problems likely to be encountered from the Health Line, but this is not always the case, and is best avoided, unless you have extensive knowledge. However, it is fair to assume that a Health Line which runs through the Life Line indicates a possible heart problem, especially if the line seems broad, in which case the problem will probably lie with circulatory difficulties. Similarly when the Health Line joins the Heart and Head Lines nervous problems are likely.

**A note of caution** A person's well-being is a delicate subject. Please make sure that you phrase any comments related to health issues carefully, so as not to cause alarm or distress. It is often best to suggest check-ups rather than to cause anxiety by making pronouncements.

## Other Features

The following diagrams show features you may come across when looking at the Health Line.

A Health Line which does not join the Life Line, indicating a robust constitution and lack of serious problems.

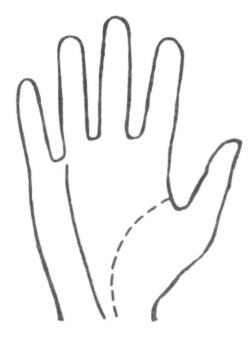

A Health Line made up of broken segments indicating problems with health throughout life.

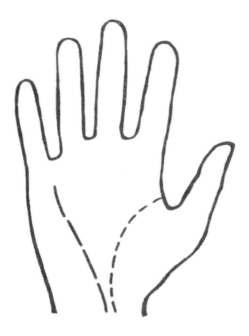

## The Sun Line

The Sun Line, also sometimes called the Line of Success, Fortune or Apollo Line, is the indicator of a person's disposition, cheerful, or not as the case may be! This is the line of potential for success, ability and talent, and is very much akin to the Fate Line. It is generally more marked on the Philosophic and Conic hands.

This is another line which may not always be apparent on a palm, but normally it runs quite close to the Fate Line (and as such is often taken as the Fate Line, or a double Fate Line) to end somewhere near the Sun Finger. If the line actually starts from the Fate Line, there is a good chance of success for the person concerned.

The line may in fact seem to start from almost anywhere, but should go towards the Mount of Apollo, hence the alternative name of Apollo' Line. It is not unusual for the Sun Line to start from the Mount of Luna (which indicates others will play a part in success), from the Head Line (indicating late success from sole efforts) or from the Heart Line (indicating a love of the arts, as well as late success). If the Fate Line and Sun Line seem to start together, it is best to see which of the two lines is the stronger. By tradition, a stronger Fate Line suggests a serious personality, whereas a stronger Sun Line suggests a more intuitive person. Again, by tradition, a well-marked Sun Line suggests a sensitive nature.

The presence of the Sun Line indicates a person who is capable and willing to work hard to fulfil their aims and to reach their targets. This is, therefore, a very good line to see on someone in a sales or a marketing position. These people are well liked and much admired. Should the Sun Line not be present, there are indications that the person will have a hard time, and anything achieved will involve a struggle. Before making any firm decisions on this, however, look at the Fate Line. A Sun Line which is clear in some places and then seems to fade out suggests temporary successes. A good Sun Line can often overcome any defects on the Fate Line.

Other Features

These diagrams show other features you may come across when looking at the Sun Line.

A Sun Line which starts between the Lines of Head and Heart and ends in a fork on Sun Mount, indicating a career which may be started in life and is not very productive.

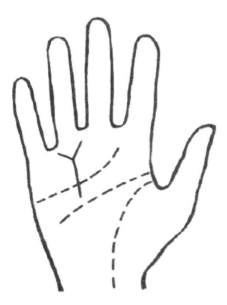

A Sun Line which starts at the wrist, goes into the Apollo Finger, indicating a very happy and productive life, with a talent for the arts.

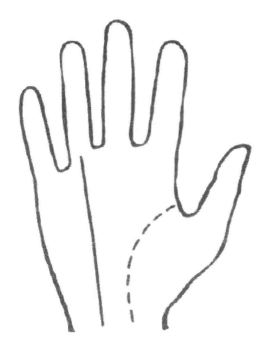

## The Girdle of Venus

The Girdle of Venus is not connected with the Mount of Venus, and may be a straight line between the first finger mount or Mount of Jupiter, and the Mercury Mount, but is normally a semicircle starting between the first and second fingers, and ending somewhere between the third and fourth fingers. It is not uncommon for the line to be short, broken, or chained, or for the line to be clear on one hand and broken on the other.

Tradition suggests the presence of this line indicates emotional sensitivity, and gives a guide to the state of the nervous system of the person concerned. However, many palmists dispute this unless the line appears on a broad hand. Normally, this line is found on those with a Conic or Psychic hand-type, who are naturally sensitive. Those people with many small crosses on the Girdle of Venus are likely to be warm, sensitive and have a love of beauty.

In Victorian times, and before, the appearance of the Girdle of Venus was said to indicate depravities, but modern palmists now suggest that in general, the line denotes someone who has acute mood swings, is temperamental, highly strung, easily upset by others, jealous, restless and prone to exaggeration. As a result, people whose hand possesses a Girdle of Venus are often subject to depression.

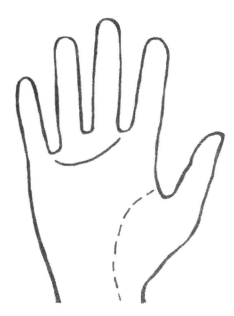

The Girdle of Venus

## Other Features

Should the line start between the first and second fingers and sweep outwards to end at the outer edge of the palm, there are indications of relationship problems, due to the mood swings. A person with a line of this nature is likely to be very difficult to live with. An example of this type of line is shown here.

The Girdle of Venus which sweeps outwards to the edge of the palm.

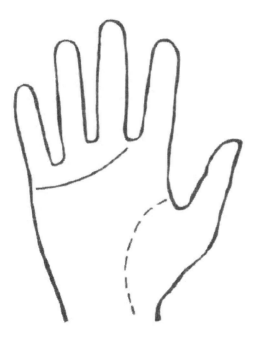

A broken Girdle of Venus, indicating a highly nervous temperament, but someone who is less jealous.

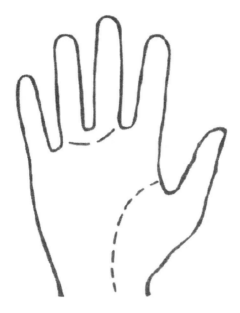

We are now going to take a look at some of the lesser lines, concentrating on the Marriage or Attachment Lines, and the Travel Lines, both of which lie towards the outer edge of the hand, and the Simian Line, a fusion of Head and Heart Lines.

## The Marriage Line or Lines

Most single people, if they are honest, are likely to have an interest in the Marriage Line.

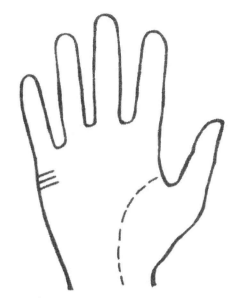

Marriage Lines.

Better called Affection Lines, Lines of Union or Affair Lines, these lines are not to be taken as indicators of a marriage, as they may indicate relationships which have been deep and long lasting, but have not resulted in marriage. Not everyone marries, but almost everyone will have these lines, irrespective of whether they have married or not. It is always necessary to look at the other lines in the hand when dealing with marriage, especially the Life Line.

Despite the fact that these lines do not necessarily indicate a marriage, for ease I will call them Marriage Lines throughout this section, but please bear in mind this might not necessarily be so.

Sometimes the Lines of Marriage will be at the side of the hand, and sometimes they will be across the front of the Mercury

Mount, but traditionally they are the small lines which enter the palm just above the Heart Line on the Mercury Mount.

Tradition suggests that a strong line shows a deep emotional attachment and a very strong, or longer, line suggests a marriage. Modern palmists merely say the stronger the line, the stronger the relationship. Any breaks in the lines suggest a split in a relationship, for one reason or another and a line which seems to curve downwards suggests the possible loss of a spouse, a long curve suggesting ill-health as the cause. Should the line curve upwards, the person is unlikely to remarry after a loss.

A line which seems to disappear would suggest separation or divorce, especially if the line forks at the end; should a second line seem to follow on, the likelihood is that there has been another relationship soon afterwards.

Should the Marriage Line seem to start near the Mount of Luna and then join the Fate Line, the marriage is likely to lack passion. A line full of splits indicates many breaks in married life.

It is said that should the Marriage Line fork off towards the Sun Line, the person concerned is likely to marry someone famous.

Many people who are not well versed in palmistry mistakenly think that the Marriage or Affection Lines indicate the number of children a person is likely to have. This is incorrect. Children are indicated by the fine, upright lines at the end of the Line of Marriage. These lines can be very fine, and it is for this reason that you should always make sure you have a magnifying glass available. Traditionally, broad lines indicate boys and lighter lines indicate girls. If one of these Children Lines is longer than the other or others, that child is likely to be the most dominant sibling. By looking to see how far apart the Children Lines appear, you can see how far apart the babies are likely to be.

However, this is a very difficult area, and in fact the whole question of children may be something to pass over quickly.

## Looking at Both Hands

The number of lines is very unlikely to be the same on the left hand
as on the right. Tradition states that the right hands suggests those
who love you and the left hand the people you yourself love. It is
said from looking at both the hands, you can work out whether there
are any unrequited love affairs!

## Timings

After wanting to know whether there is a marriage or strong attachment indicated in the palm, most people will want to know at what time that attachment is to be formed. In all honesty, this is not an easy thing to gauge, but roughly, you should count the age upwards from the Heart Line. If you divide the line by 4, that quarter point indicates anywhere from 18-25. Halfway between the Heart Line and the finger indicates 25-30 and after that it will be over 30.

# Travel Lines

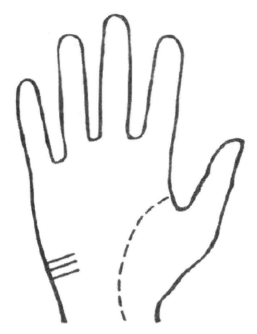

Travel Lines

These lines do not play a prominent part in palmistry, but again many people seem to want to know whether they are likely to travel, especially as it is now so easy to travel to far-away places.

These lines, like the Marriage or Affection Lines, are short lines. They normally appear, if they appear at all, on the outer edge of the hand just below the Heart Line on the Mount of Luna.

Normally longer than the Marriage Lines, they indicate whether a journey will be important or not, and whether the travel is merely likely to concern holidays or something a little more permanent. In general terms, the longer the line, the more important the journey.

Should the Travel Line actually join the Heart line, it is said that the journey will involve romance. Should the Travel Line meet up with the Fate Line, the journey will prove financially beneficial. If the Travel Line joins the Head Line and then breaks, there may be illness associated with the journey.

## Other Features

When looking for indications of travel, also look for any small lines running from the Life Line but keeping level with it. This could look a little like a long fork coming from the Life Line. Such lines also indicate journeys of a very important nature, and could even indicate emigration. You should also look at the Bracelets around the wrist. Should the first Bracelet rise into the Mount of Luna, there is likely to be travel and many journeys.

# The Simian Line

This is a fused line of Head and Heart, which crosses the palm and seems to cut the hand into two sections. It is not a line which appears on all palms, but its presence indicates someone who is unable to relax or switch off, someone who is restless and likely to wake up in the middle of the night thinking of new projects. This person often takes up many hobbies to channel their energies. This is someone who is determined to succeed, no matter what, and has a power of concentration which is unequalled. This person will be shrewd and clever, but ruthless and immature. They do not believe in moderating their energies, never think that they are in the wrong, and on occasions may come close to breaking the law.

People with a Simian Line may have difficulty making friends or forming relationships, probably due to their over-powering personality.

Tradition suggests someone with a Simian Line should not be trusted, as the Heart Line governs emotions and the Head Line controls intellect and a fusion weakens the balance. There needs to be a gap between the Head and Heart Lines for a person to be able to reason logically.

Usually, a Simian Line, if present at all, will only appear on one hand, although occasionally it will be seen in both hands, in which case it is likely to show an egocentric, blinkered, personality. It is fair to say that should the line be present on both hands, the person is likely to be exceptionally intelligent and yet lack in imagination and feel frustrated, due to his intellect only being partly utilised.

Normally, a Simian Line which is low set shows a passionate and intense person whose power of reasoning is likely to be employed; a high Simian Line indicates a more emotional person with less intellectual ability.

A high-set Simian Line.

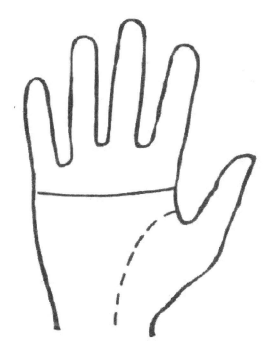

A low-set Simian Line.

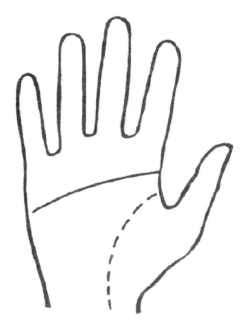

A thin Simian Line is rarer than a thick one, and generally the thinner the line, the more active the person. Should the line be thicker at the outer edge of the palm, the emotions are likely to be instinctive, whereas a line which is thicker towards the thumb shows a calculating person. A materialistic outlook is shown when the Simian Line is thick and broad and runs straight across the palm.

## Practice

We are now going to be answering questions on some of the lines we have looked at in this chapter, and again, no answers are given.

- What is another name for the Fate Line?
- Give the other names for the Health Line.

- Where does the Girdle of Venus lie on the palm?
- Does everyone have Attachment or Marriage Lines?
- Where does a good Fate Line start and end?
- What does it mean when there are bars across the Fate Line?
- Does everyone have a Health Line?
- What is a Simian Line, and does everyone have one?
- What major characteristics would apply to someone with a Simian Line?
- What did the Victorians think a person with the Girdle of Venus on their palm was likely to be?

# CHAPTER 4 – The Mounts

This chapter's emphasis is on the mounts of the hand, and in particular those of Jupiter, Saturn, Apollo, Mercury, Moon, Neptune and Venus. We will then go on to look at what is known as the Zone of Mars. Mounts are as important a part of palmistry as the lines, and a close inspection of the mounts is always necessary when embarking on a palmistry reading.

## What are Mounts?

The mounts are the fleshy pads beneath the fingers, at the base of the thumb and along the edge of the palm. Each mount indicates various character traits, and each mount is different.

The names given to these mounts are those of the seven principal planets in our solar system and were given to the mounts by the Greeks, who associated various characteristics with the planets.

## What to Look for

In general terms, mounts should be firm but not hard, and be well developed. In order to assess what sort of mount you are looking at, it is necessary to touch the area lightly with your fingers so you can feel whether it is firm or soft.

The diagram on the next page shows the mounts, which, as you will see, relate to the fingers in some respects, the Mount of Jupiter being below the Jupiter Finger etc. There is also an area or zone known as the Zone of Mars, which incorporates the Plain of Mars, as well an Upper and Lower Mars.

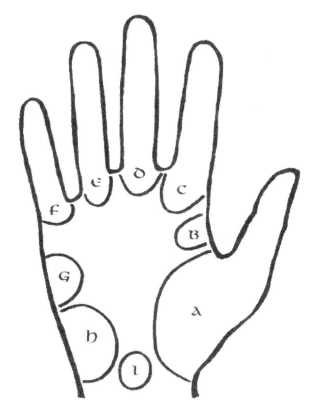

A = Venus
B = Lower Mars
C = Jupiter
D = Saturn
E = Apollo
F = Mercury
G =Upper Mars
H = Luna
I = Neptune

We will start by looking at the digital mounts, that is those mounts below the fingers.

It is important to remember when looking at mounts to look for other indications on the lines of the palm. As we go through each mount, the line to look at in addition to the mount itself is also given.

## Jupiter Mount

This area falls immediately below the index or Jupiter Finger, and relates to ambition and leadership. When looking at any mount, it is important to determine whether the mount seems rounded and in proportion to the other mounts, is prominent, or underdeveloped, as different characteristics apply to each of these types.

It is also important to look at both hands, and in the case of Mount of Jupiter, you should also look at the Head Line.

### In Proportion

Proud, well balanced, a social animal, with confidence and self-respect. This person is likely to be ambitious, active, and may also be quite religious. They are also likely to be well organised.

### Prominent

Conceited, overbearing and selfish. This person may be quite Draconian and arrogant.

### Under developed

Lacking in self-respect, inconsistent, lazy, shrewd and self-indulgent. There may be a tendency towards depression, especially if the mount is hollow or flat, when the person is likely to be a natural worrier.

## Saturn Mount

This area falls beneath the middle or Saturn Finger, and relates to study, stability and mental fortitude. When looking at the Mount of Saturn, also look at the Fate Line.

### In Proportion

Liking their own space and peace and quiet, this person is likely to love nature and be good in the garden. Kind, serious, self-controlled, truthful, considerate and dutiful, they are very independent, and will fight any restrictions which curb their need for freedom of action.

### Prominent

Melancholic, morbid, and easily upset by others, these people are inclined towards depression and mood swings. They are often very interested in the arts.

### Under Developed

Frivolous, nervous and somewhat vindictive, this is not a good sign to see on a hand.

## Apollo Mount

Also known as the Sun Mount, this area falls beneath the third or Apollo Finger, and relates to creativity and artistic leanings. When looking at the Apollo Mount, also look at the Sun Line.

## In Proportion

Happy, helpful, generous, sympathetic and cheerful. Despite being able to cheer up other people, often these people are unable to lift their own moods. They are by nature, kind, loving and sincere, and may be talented in music or the arts, despite their conventional approach. It is best to look at the Venus Mount here also.

## Prominent

It is often considered to be very fortunate to have a well-developed Apollo Mount. These people are enthusiastic, happy, generous and able to rise to great heights; they like attention, and may go all out to seek it. They can, unfortunately, also be susceptible to flattery, extravagant and rash. People with excessive Apollo Mounts are fond of any form of speculation or gambling.

## Under developed

Self-conscious, shy, and sometimes dull, these people do well in business despite themselves, probably because they are better before an audience, when they can act a part rather than being themselves. They can be mean with money and seem cruel at times, when their temper gets the better of them.

# Mercury Mount

This area is beneath the little or Mercury Finger, and relates to the mind, and to mental abilities. When looking at this mount, also look at the Head and Health Lines.

## In Proportion

Intelligent, restless and changeable, these people are extremely good in business situations, being active, shrewd and industrious. Cheerful and talkative, they should be allowed to have freedom for self-expression.

## Prominent

Chatterboxes, sometimes unaware that they upset others, they can be moody, ambitious and cunning, and find it easy to lie.

## Under developed

Lacking in initiative and assertiveness, these people often lack a sense of humour and are lethargic and unimaginative.

We will now look at the mounts connected to other parts of the palm. These too have names which relate to planets within our solar system.

## Moon or Luna Mount

This is the area near the base of the outer edge of the palm, between the Head Line and the wrist, and relates to imagination and intuition. It can also be linked with a person's psychic abilities, personal needs and communication skills. Should the Luna Mount seem to link in with the Venus Mount, there is

likely to be a passionate person there! If the Venus Mount, seems to encroach
upon the Luna Mount, however, there are likely to be wasted energies. When looking at the Luna Mount, look to see if there is an Intuition Line, which we will learn about in Chapter 5.

## In Proportion

Imaginative and original. This person needs harmony and balance to operate effectively and is likely to be creative, affectionate, lively and probably very interested in spirituality.

## Prominent

Eccentric, very imaginative and romantic, these people are idealists, who love travel and change. They can be inconsistent and frivolous, especially in affairs of the heart. They are likely to be jealous and suffer from nervous problems.

## Under Developed

Lacking in imagination, these people are often religious and charitable, finding pleasure in helping others. They have fixed opinions on duty, and can appear secretive and timid. They view with scepticism anything which they don't fully understand.

## Neptune Mount

Considered to be a relatively new mount, this mount is not traditional, but was added to palmistry following the discovery of the planet Neptune last century. It is found between the mounts of Venus and Luna at the base of the palm, and relates to instinct. As with the Luna Mount, look also at the Intuition Line, if one is present.

### In Proportion

Lively and full of fun, this person is likely to sail through most difficulties.

### Prominent

A magnetic personality, with theatrical tendencies which should be encouraged, this person is likely to be happy surrounded by other people who take pleasure in listening, rather than speaking.

### Under Developed

Indifferent towards the needs and demands of other people, this person is likely to seem aloof and cold, preferring solitude to being in a crowd. Any difficulties will be dealt with in a clear and precise way, with little fuss or sign of emotion.

## Venus Mount

This is the fleshy pad at the base of the thumb, inside the Life Line, and relates to energy and health matters, as well as to emotional and physical needs. When looking at the Venus Mount, also look at the Heart Line for further clarification.

### In Proportion

Warm, affectionate, charitable, active and generous, this person is likely to be very keen on sports and passionate about most things, especially music, and be artistic and emotional.

## Prominent

Sensual and magnetic, this person also is likely to be keen on music and the arts, and probably has a good singing voice. Impulsive, often outspoken and hot-tempered, this person can be vain and egotistical.

## Under Developed

Cold and lacking in energy, this person is likely to be inhibited, yet have pronounced psychic abilities and a keen intuition. Traditional and self-controlled, this person is often restless and unhappy.

We have now covered the major mounts with the exception of the Zone of Mars, which is broken down into three separate segments:

Upper Mars, Lower Mars and the Plain of Mars. These areas need to be looked at together, rather than in isolation, as they are closely linked.

# Upper Mars

This is located immediately above the Luna Mount, close to the Mercury Mount. Some palmists call this mount the Negative Mars when large, and you may come across this term should you undertake further study of palmistry. This area relates to mental energy and 'staying power'.

## Prominent

These people are clever, cunning people, very determined and versatile. There is unlimited staying power here and ambitions are high. These people are likely to be very active, impetuous and hot tempered.

## Under developed

In the unlikely event that this area is hollow or under-developed, the person concerned is likely to exhibit shy and cowardly tendencies.

## Lower Mars

This is located near the Life Line, above the Mount of Venus. Some palmists call this mount the Positive Mars when large. The area relates to passion, aggression and physical energy levels. It is wise to also look at the Life Line when considering this area.

### Prominent

These people are dogmatic and have firm views, disliking and resenting criticism. They have a lot of physical energy, which should ideally be channelled into exercise to provide a release valve. Generous, obstinate and lacking in self-control, these people often overspend and over-indulge. It is very rare that both Lower and Upper Mars will be large, and it is again wise to look at both hands, as the chances of both hands showing prominent Mars Mounts is unlikely. However, should both mounts be prominent, the person concerned is likely to be indifferent, shy, unimaginative and nervous, with mild manners and behaviour.

## Plain of Mars

This area lies in the centre of the palm. Within this area is what is sometimes called the Great Triangle, which is the intersection of the lines of the Head, Life and Mercury, and the Quadrangle, which is the area between the Heart and Head Lines. Professional palmists will divide these areas still further into Lower, Middle and Upper Angles. However, it is not necessary to do so here. The Plain of Mars gives indications on the general energy levels a person possesses.

## Prominent

It is often difficult to gauge whether the Plain of Mars is well developed, or not, and it is vital that the area be tested by touch. Most people would seem, on initial inspection, to have a flat Plain of Mars, but when you touch the area, you can see whether it is hard or springy. Tradition suggests that a developed Plain of Mars should be firm and full, and this would indicate a great deal of energy, an interest in politics and a resourceful and active lifestyle.

## Under developed

Should the area, however, be thin and under-developed, the person is likely to have little interest in the world and be generally lazy.

A note of caution :
Make sure that you look at the lines on the palm and other signs when dealing with information obtained from the mounts. You should never make judgements without looking at the whole picture.

## The Zodiac Link

As you will see from the above diagram and from what we have discussed so far, there is a strong connection between palmistry and astrology, and in ancient times the two were studied together.

Many palmists who are well versed in astrology and able to draw up birth charts for comparison purposes will give astrological names to areas on the palm. For instance, traditional astrological palmists would say that Aries is placed on the Mount of Neptune, Taurus on the Mount of Venus, Gemini at the base of the Mount of Jupiter, the next three signs on the Jupiter Finger, on the third, second and first phalanges respectively, and the next three signs on the Apollo Finger in the same way, ending with Capricorn on the base of Apollo Mount, Aquarius on the upper part of Luna Mount, and Pisces on the lower part of the Luna Mount.

Some palmists who follow more modern schools of thought will give the various hand-types different element qualities, and will refer to them as Air Hand rather than simply calling them Square Hand etc.

## Practice

This set of questions will concern the mounts, as this has been the main emphasis of this chapter.

• Where is the Neptune Mount?
• What does it mean when we come across someone with a highly-developed Upper Mars?
• What line should we also look at when looking at Jupiter Mount?
• We are looking at a hand with a prominent Saturn Mount. What does this indicate?
• How should we judge the Plain of Mars for development?
• We are providing a map of the hand showing the astrological symbols relating to the mounts.

# CHAPTER 5 – Smaller Lines and Rings

When we were looking at mounts in the last chapter, reference was made to Intuition Lines and we are now going to have a look at some of these smaller lines, and also at the Rings.

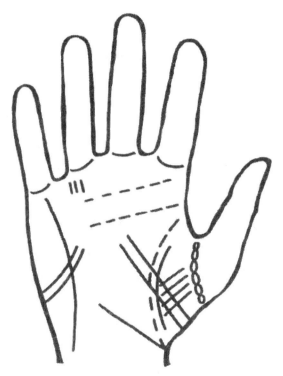

It is important to realise that not everyone will have all the lines mentioned here. Some people may have a line on one hand or both, and others none at all. Don't fall into the trap of looking for lines that might not be there and deciding they must be there but you can't see them. If you look carefully and don't see them, the chances are they aren't there!

## The Intuition Line

Also known as the Line of Inspiration or sometimes as Via Lasciva, (perhaps incorrectly, as some palmists suggest a different line for this name) this is one of the lesser lines which may not appear on all hands, or be only barely visible.

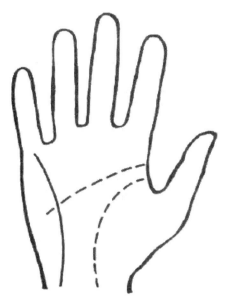

Usually found near the Luna Mount, starting on or near to the wrist, it sometimes looks like a semi-circular Health Line, and ends on the Mount of Mercury. Because of its proximity to the Health Line, some palmists refer to it as a Sister Health Line.

The appearance of this line shows a person with intuition, good perception and foresight. It would be wrong to assume from this that there is also a psychic ability, as this may not be so, although it is possible. These people are likely to experience vivid dreams and be blessed with abundant energy.

Most often this line will appear on those with a Philosophic, Conic or Psychic Hand. The person concerned is likely to be very impressionable and sensitive, have a good memory, especially remembering things seen, be nervous and possibly unable to cope well with set-backs, as well as possessing good judgement of others from first meeting. This is someone who really can 'judge a book by its cover'.

Traditionally, if there is no intuition line on the right hand and only a weak one on the left, the person has inherited a 'sixth sense' but chosen to ignore its presence or decided against using this natural psychic ability.

## The Loyalty Line

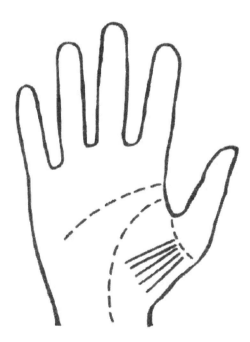

This is not really one line but a series of small lines, close together, which lie within the Mount of Venus, from the middle of the base of the thumb.

These lines (or line) concern the family and suggest a close family unit or family ties. Those with a particularly strong Loyalty Line are likely to be very close to their parents and grandparents, and even cousins, uncles and aunts. The family will be important.

Often people who have Loyalty Lines will find themselves working in family businesses or involved with the family in a large way. It is often interesting to see how many men working as part of a family business have these lines. Calling them Loyalty Lines can often cause men in particular to question the palmist, as they may see the fact that they work in the family business as not a question of loyalty, but something into which they were drawn without much chance of opposition!

Should one of these Loyalty Lines touch or cut into the Life Line, there is likely to have been a particularly strong relationship with one or other parent, and the individual concerned will take every opportunity to talk about the family and will attach great importance to the family unit. (Please note, it makes no difference if a person has been adopted; the word 'family' usually suggests natural family, but where someone has been adopted or has lost their biological parents, this refers to a close bonding with someone who became important from their earliest memories.)

Should all the Loyalty Lines seem to touch the Life Line, the person concerned is likly to be quite fanatical about his or her family, and will vigorously defend its members, if necessary. It is very possible that, upon marriage, the spouse's family will become important also, but the person's own family will always come first.

# The Family Ring

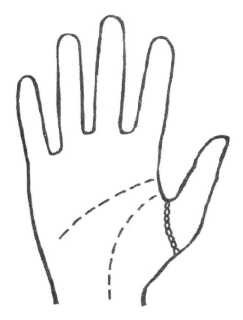

This is the line which seems to divide the thumb from the Mount of Venus. Sometimes it is known as the Ring of Venus for this reason. It is rarely a 'cutting line', and more likely a series of lines or chains, some heavier than others, dividing the second phalange of the thumb from the Venus Mount.

This line, when heavy and obvious, shows strong family loyalties, and has an obvious relationship with the Loyalty Lines, which originate from within this area. If the line is faint, there are likely to be few family loyalties or relationships.

On some hands, you may find that the line is more clearly defined at the top of the thumb than at the bottom. This is normally found on the palm of those whose family ties have reduced over the years.

## Influence Lines and Mounts

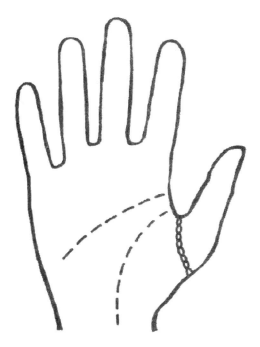

The lines which run down the Mount of Venus usually start from the Life Line and keep close to it.

These lines relate to people who mean a great deal to the owner of the hand, such as a brother, sister, or close friend, rather than a more passionate relationship.

An Influence Line which seems to run close to the start of the Life Line but not touch it, is likely to indicate someone who was very important in childhood, especially if the line then moves away from the Life Line. This would suggest that as the owner of the hand matured, the friendship became less important.

Should these influence lines actually cut across the Life Line and go into the Line of Destiny, the influence will be from a blood relationship. Traditionally, an influence line which cuts both Life and Destiny Lines is more powerful than an Influence Line which stops at the Life Line.

Influence Lines which cut into the Head Line or Heart Line show that family have been influential in career or personal relationships. Broken Influence Lines relate to arguments, separations or other problems.

Influence Lines which run from the Luna Mount may also run into the Fate Line, and relate to help given in a career situation by friends or family. Should these influence lines extend to the Line of Destiny, indications are that others have been influential in the destiny of the owner in some way or other. If they stop at the Line of Destiny rather than cutting into it, the indications are favourable.

Some palmists maintain that it is possible to judge love affairs from the Influence Lines, and this is indeed so, but it is also important to refer to the affection Lines.

Influence Lines from the Luna Mount to the Destiny Line.

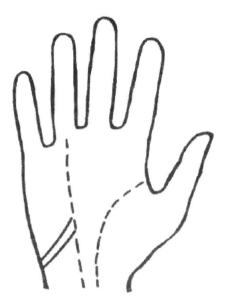

Influence Lines from the Venus Mount cutting the Head Line.

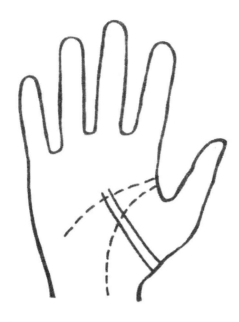

## The Line of Mars

This line, sometimes known as the Inner Life Line, seems to support the Life Line, and runs within the Life Line on the Mount of Venus, sometimes starting from Lower Mars. This line is rare, but, when visible, runs parallel to, and inside, the Life Line.

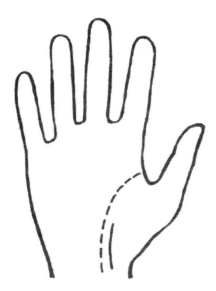

This line relates to a person's resilience to withstand illness and shock. If the Life Line in that area seems to show illnesses or problems (be broken, for example), the presence of the Line of Mars will modify the difficulties, especially if the hand-type is Philosophical or Conic.

Should this line be found on a broad-handed person, or someone with a Squared Hand-type, the person is likely to have very good health and a strong constitution, and be able to withstand any difficulties with ease.

Should there be a fork on the Line of Mars which seems to go towards the Luna Mount, the person concerned is, by tradition, likely to need variety and excitement, and be hot-tempered.

## Via Lascivia

As already mentioned, some palmists give this name to the Line of Intuition. However, the line to which we now refer is the semi-circular line which normally runs from the base of the Luna Mount towards the Mount of Venus. This line can, however, have other positions, such as running from the lower part of the Luna Mount towards the wrist, as shown here.

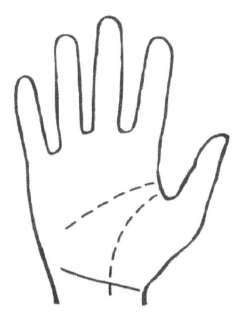

Sometimes known as the Drink Line, this is quite rare, and relates to people who have a high energy level but intolerances or allergies to certain substances, such as wine, beer or drugs. If this line is present on a hand, the person concerned should be advised to watch their food and liquid intake, and to take up a sport which would utilise their surplus energy.

## Medical Stigmata

These lines again are by no means apparent on all palms, and are normally lines which are located close to the Mercury Finger, slightly above the Heart Line.

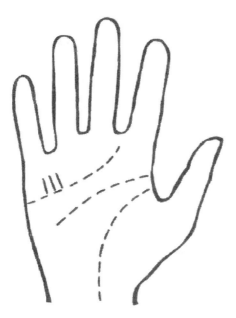

These lines relate to a person with healing capabilities, either in the field of orthodox or complementary medicine.

Sometimes, people with these marks will be 'Good Samaritan' types, who like to help other people, whilst in other cases they may show a person who is actually working in a healing profession.

## The Ring of Apollo

This is a line which is very rarely seen, but runs at the top of the Mount of Apollo at the base of the Apollo Finger. Although this line indicates poor judgement, it is necessary to look at the hand itself before making a firm decision on this.

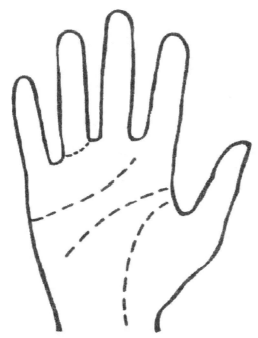

If the hand is poor, or the Apollo Finger is poorly developed, the person is certainly likely to suffer from bad taste or poor judgement. On a well-developed hand or finger, however, the person concerned is likely to have talents in entertainment or the arts, and possibly have career difficulties.

## The Ring of Mercury

Another line seldom seen, but which is often a series of broken lines which curve around the base of the Mercury Finger at the top of the Mercury Mount.

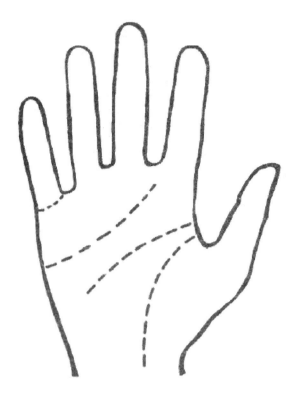

The presence of this line is believed to give the owner a good head for business. However, this depends to a large extent on the type of hand on which the line appears. In a -poorly-developed hand, the person is likely to be a little unethical in business; on a well-developed hand, the person is likely to be determined and ambitious.

Tradition suggests that the presence of this line indicates a person who will have little desire to marry, but still have plenty of relationships!

## The Ring of Saturn

This line curves around the base of the Saturn Finger at the top of the Saturn Mount, and again is likely to be formed by a series of broken lines.

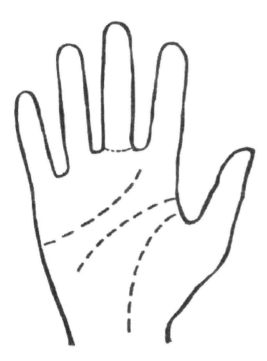

The person possessing this line is likely to be a loner, preferring his own company to that of others, but not to the extreme of living a hermit-like existence.

This person often seems dull and boring and tends to appear cut off from his environment.

## The Ring of Solomon

This line curves around the base of the Jupiter Finger at the top of the Jupiter Mount, and is often called the Jupiter Ring for this reason.

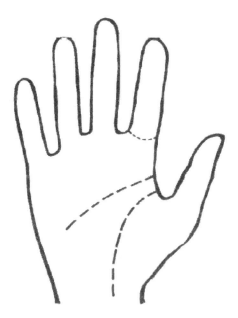

This is the mark of the teacher, someone with the ability to absorb information and pass it on, especially if the Jupiter Finger is straight and well developed. People with this mark often become figures of authority within the community, and have an interest in the law and philosophy. If the Jupiter Finger seems poorly developed, however, the person may take part in underhand business deals, which could lead to trouble.

## Practice

We have now looked at many of the minor lines and the Rings at the base of the fingers, and will be answering questions on some of the topics discussed.

- Associated with wisdom, which Ring is found at the base of the Jupiter Finger?
- What is another name for the Sister Health Line?
- The Family Ring and Loyalty Line are in the same area of the hand. On which mount are they found?
- Influence Lines can run from two mounts. Which two?
- Where would you expect to find Medical Stigmata, and what do these lines mean?
- On what hand-types would you expect to find the Intuition Line, if at all?

# CHAPTER 6 – Marks

In this chapter we will be looking at double lines, small marks, and stress-related signs.

## Double Lines

Sometimes called Sister Lines, these lines are those which seem to run parallel to a major line for part or its entire course.

Do not think that these double lines are often seen, because this is far from the case. However, when such lines are visible, the secondary line often seems to be acting as a support line for a weakened major line.

A double or Sister Line would look something like this:

An example of this would be if the major line, say the Heart Line, shows breaks, chains or forks; a double, or secondary, Heart Line would serve to help to strengthen the line.

Sometimes these lines are also apparent when the major line seems to be quite strong. However, this is not always the case, and it would be best for you to look carefully at the major line before making any firm decisions. If, however, the main line does appear strong, the secondary line is likely to show an alternative attitude or thought pattern from that indicated by the main line.

## Small Marks

There are a number of small marks which can appear on a hand, and these are:

The Cross

The Star

The Square

The Island

The Circle

The Dot, or Spot

The Mystic, St Andrew's, or Psychic Cross

The Grille

The Triangle

The Chain

The Tassel

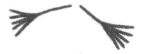

The Bar

When these signs appear, they can be both good and bad signs. As we look at each mark, we will discuss this further, but generally speaking, circles, squares, triangles and stars are beneficial when found on any of the Mounts on the palm, whereas dots (or spots), islands, crosses, grilles, bars, tassels and chains are not.

The Mystic Cross, or Psychic Cross does not fall into either of these good/bad categories, but, traditionally, indicates psychic ability.

It is wise to look at the whole area of the palm, and the area round the mark before making any firm decisions as to whether the mark is beneficial or not. As with any feature on the palm, it is unwise to look at it in isolation - it would be like suggesting you know the plot of a novel when you have read one page.

## The Cross

As already stated, this is seldom a favourable sign, as it indicates loss, problems, troubles and disappointments, and is said to weaken any line it touches. The one exception to this is when there is a cross on the Mount of Jupiter, which suggests a love link or even marriage, especially if linked to a star, and if the Fate Line starts from the Luna Mount.

A cross is basically two lines of opposite energies meeting, and looks, something like this:

There are various places where you may find a cross, or crosses. Amongst these are the following, with traditional meanings:

On Saturn Mount
If touching the Fate Line, there are likely to be accidents. If in the centre of the Mount on its own, the danger may be less.

On Apollo Mount
Disappointments in achievements or desires.

On Mercury Mount
Dishonesty.

On Mars Mount

If under Mercury, opposition is indicated, if under Jupiter, violence is suggested.

On Luna Mount
Under the Head Line, this is a sign of deceit. If moving in to the Plain of Mars, there will be journeys by sea.
On Venus Mount
Very great problems if heavily marked, but if small and near the Life Line, problems with close relatives.

Surrounded by a square
Protection from attack, possibly from an animal.

Over the Heart Line
The loss of someone close.

By the Fate Line
Between the Fate Line and Line of Mars, there will be family problems which could affect the career or ultimate destiny. If next to the Luna Mount, there will be travel disappointments.

Touching the Fate Line
Money difficulties.

First nail phalange, Saturn Finger
 An interest in animals or animal welfare.

Touching the Head Line
Accident(s) to the head area.

By the Sun Line
Disappointments in job-related matters.


## The Star

This can be a more fortunate sign, but one which depends upon the area in which it is found. The star relates to added energy, or even shock, and looks like this:

The star is often less perfectly formed than illustrated here, and can be made up of lots of small lines which seem to meet in the middle.

It is one of the lesser signs to look for, and you may never come across one at all.

There are various places where you might find a star or stars, some of which are as follows:

On the fingers
Provided the star is on the finger tips or outer phalanges, this is a good sign, especially if on the thumb, when success will be apparent through determination and will-power.

On the Mount of Luna
Ancient teachings suggest that this means a drowning, but more modern thought suggests a dreamer or unrealistic attitude, or even mental disturbance.

On the Head Line
A mental shock.

At the end of the Fate Line or Sun Line
Success and an eventful yet varied lifetime, maybe even one of danger.

On the Mount of Venus
Success in affairs of the heart.

On the Life Line
A possible injury.

On the Heart Line
Possibly a heart problem, or an emotional trauma.

On Upper Mars
Success through perseverance.

On Lower Mars
Success in a physical pursuit or service career.

On the three major lines
A bad shock to the system which will change the person completely.

A star on the other mounts merely intensifies the qualities of the mount.

## The Square

This is a good sign in most cases, and is usually found close to, or surrounding, another mark or break. Sometimes the square is known as the Mark of Preservation, because it protects from dangers indicated by other lines or marks.

A square can be made of major or minor lines or both, and looks like this:

There are, again, various places where a square might be found, and these include the following:

On the Fate Line
Crisis, but the outcome will not be total ruin or loss.

On the Head Line
Stresses, anxiety or work-related problems.

On the Heart Line
Problems due to emotions.

On the Life Line
Health problems, but not too serious.

When found on any of the mounts, any excess negativities from that mount will be weakened. However, Jupiter Mount, which concerns ambitions, is different. A square on Jupiter Mount suggests a talent for teaching, and is sometimes known as the Teacher's Square. If this links also with a triangle, the person is likely to be very communicative and an effective speaker.

## Islands

The island is not a fortunate sign. Again its meanings depend upon the line on which it is found. Islands hardly ever appear anywhere other than on a line. Should an island be found on a mount, the qualities of that mount are weakened.

Traditionally, islands were said to relate to hereditary problems, and look like this:

There are various places where an island may be found, and these include the following:

On the Heart Line
Physical problems, which can be further defined by looking at the area of the Heart Line affected. Under Saturn - hearing problems, under Mercury ....problems with the teeth, under Apollo - problems with eyesight, on the Heart Line - can indicate a heart weakness, especially if the island appears at the start of the Heart Line.

On the Head Line Mental strain

On the Life Line Illness or weak constitution. It is important to look at the timing of this problem, and see how long it is likely to
continue, as, generally speaking, it will exist for as long as the line is
divided. Someone who had problems at birth will have an island at
the start of their Life Line.

Any small line which contains an island suggests scandal or disgrace. For example, should a line form an island and then join up with the Marriage or Affection Lines, indications are that there will be disgrace within the marriage at that point. A line which ends in an island is also a bad sign, indicating problems which will weaken any positivity shown by the line. Islands on any mounts weaken the qualities of the mount.

## The Circle

A rarely seen but fortunate marking. A true circle should look something like this, and should not be confused with an island, which only appears on a line:

There are various places where a circle might be found, and these include the following:

On Luna Mount
Traditionally danger from water, even drowning.

On Apollo Mount
Talent, even genius, depending upon the rest of the hand.

On the Heart
Line Eyesight difficulties, especially if under the Apollo Mount; if under the Saturn Mount, hearing difficulties are likely.

When touching any of the major lines, a circle indicates problems which will be difficult to resolve.

## The Dot

Sometimes also called the Spot or Crater, dots are generally a sign of temporary illness, health difficulties, or delays. Dots look something like this:

Dots normally only appear on lines, and can be found in several places including the following:

On the Head Line
Headaches, sinus problems, migraines, problems with the head generally.

On the Heart Line
Problems in the chest area. If under the Saturn Finger, problems with digestion, and if under the Mercury Finger, problems with lungs or breathing.

On the Life Line
Back or spinal problems, but if lower down on the Life Line, kidney or bladder problems are indicated, and if near the bottom of the Life Line, mobility problems are suggested.

Traditionally, you should also look at the colour of the spot, as red spots are linked to physical health and blue or black spots to nervous or mental problems.


## The Psychic Cross

This is a strange mark, which, traditionally is said to indicate second-sight or psychic tendencies. The Psychic Cross is normally found in the middle of the palm, and looks something like this:

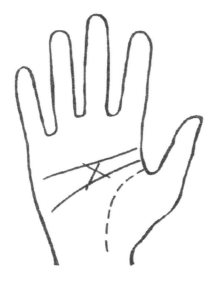

Also known as the St. Andrew's Cross, Croix Mystique or Mystic Cross, it is normally found between the Head and Heart Lines, but not touching either. It can be formed by the Fate Line and a line from the Head to the Heart Lines, or it can lie completely isolated away from all the major lines.

The Psychic Cross, suggesting an interest in the occult, mysticism or superstition, can have slightly different meanings, depending on its location. It may be found in the following areas:

Under the Saturn Finger
An active interest in psychic matters.

Near Jupiter Mount
A belief in the mystic but not to a great extent. This person will probably have an interest in 'the future' but have no talents to develop and no wish to acquire any. If, however, the mark appears on Jupiter Mount, the person is likely to want to develop any talents for personal use.

Close to the Heart Line
Superstitious.

Over the Head Line
Very superstitious and with a very great interest in psychic matters.

Touching the Fate Line
This could be someone who is already, or is capable of, working within the psychic field, and may well make this their career.

A feature to look for Look to see if there is a Ring of Solomon should you find a Psychic Cross on a palm. If so, the person is likely to be highly talented and possibly well known in the psychic field.

## The Grille

Fairly common, and generally found upon the mounts of the hand, especially on Venus Mount. The grille indicates obstacles and looks something like this:

In addition to the mounts, it is possible to find the grille on lines, but normally only at the end of a line, when it weakens the strength of the line. However, when found on the mounts, the meanings are as follows:

On Jupiter Mount Selfish personality, proud, egotistical and dominating. This is said to indicate the troublemaker in our midst.

On Venus Mount A passionate person who is wasteful with energies.

On Saturn Mount A depressive person subject to misfortunes and lacking in purpose.

On Apollo Mount Vanity, a desire to be the centre of attention, and an abnormally high self-esteem.

On Mercury Mount Instability, ill-judged belief that other people can be easily taken in and duped. A total lack of principles.

On Luna Mount Sensitive and restless, this indicates someone who is seldom happy. Should the Health Line pass through the grille, the person is likely to suffer extreme highs and lows emotionally.

## The Triangle

Another strange mark, which is not formed by crossing lines, and business, also likely to indicate a political person. is often very clear. However, should this not be the case, be sure you are looking at a triangle and not a square. A true triangle looks like this:

Sometimes you may see something that looks like a spearhead or tripod. This is not a triangle, but is a good sign indicating successes.

A triangle can appear on any mount, and indicates talents, both mental and physical.

Triangles usually appear on mounts only, but very occasionally appear on a line, and should this be the case, the positive qualities of line will be weakened but not destroyed. When appearing on the
mounts, the following meanings apply:

On Jupiter Mount
Excellent management potential, diplomacy and organisational talents.

On Saturn Mount
An investigative nature, the sign of the student of mankind. Look to see if the Head Line is short, as these two signs indicate someone who is likely to be interested in superstitions and anything mystical.

On Apollo Mount
Creative, constructive, calm and successful, with an artistic leaning, especially towards architecture or something practical.

On Mars Mount
Someone who never gives up, has a 'fighting spirit', is calm in crisis situations, and who will carry the banner for a cause. If the triangle appears on Lower Mars the person will show a calm presence of mind in an emergency or dangerous situation.

On Luna Mount
Balance and good judgement, with a logical manner and imaginative ideas.

On Neptune Mount
Psychic abilities are indicated.

On Venus Mount

Self-restrained and calm.

On Mercury Mount
Clear thinking and an excellent head for business, also likely to indicate a political person.

## The Chain

Sometimes also called garlands, these lines weaken the strength of the line on which they are found, but only for as long as they actually appear on the line. The chain may look something like this:

Under the Head Line
Migraines are indicated.

On the Life Line
A sign of bad health, and particularly if the hand is soft. The health of the person will improve once the line continues.

## The Tassel

This is basically a line which has forked into many small branches, and is normally found at the end of a line. It looks something like this:

Again it weakens the line, and indicates deterioration with age. More often than not, it will be found on the Health and Life Lines.

## The Bar

This looks like a line or lines which cut across a major line, and will look something like this:

The bar acts as a barrier, and blocks the positivity of the line at that point. Sometimes it is called a Delaying Bar. Traditionally, these delays are the things which we will remember in the future.

## Stress, Strains and Frustrations

All of us, irrespective of age, sex, career, marital status or intelligence will suffer from frustrations of one sort or another during our lifetimes. Sometimes these frustrations will lead to stress-related illnesses, whether they be migraines, digestive problems or something more serious. Such signs will show up on the hand, but it is important to remember that it is inadvisable to diagnose a health problem, and unless you are medically qualified, you should never make specific diagnoses or cause alarm.

Stresses and strains show up both on the lines of the palm and on the finger-nails.

Let's look at the Life Line, for instance. We have already seen that breaks in the Life Line can indicate temporary illnesses or general ill health.

Signs of hormonal difficulties will show up as lines running across the fingertips. General exhaustion, stress or feeling run-down will show up as vertical lines running up and down the fingers, sometimes also called White Lines. These lines normally are confined to the first phalange. Taking a look at the fingers in particular, you can generally make the following assessments:

On the Jupiter Finger
Personal and financial insecurities and anxieties.

On the Saturn Finger
Definite monetary worries and/or career difficulties.

On the Apollo Finger
Emotional problems.

On the Mercury Finger
Communication problems leading to relationship difficulties.

You should also look to see whether the lines on the hand are clear or not.

Stress will also be indicated by a badly-formed Girdle of Venus.

Someone with a lot of fine lines on their palm is likely to be a nervous person, more subject to stress than someone with fewer lines.

Frustrations show up on the middle and lower phalanges. The meanings are as follows:

On the Jupiter Finger
The problem is likely to be related to ambition or religious convictions.

On the Saturn Finger
The problem is related to relationships.

On the Apollo Finger
The problem relates to creative interests.

On the Mercury Finger
The problem relates to career or communication difficulties.

## Stress and the Nails

Look also to the nails for information on stress. White flecks on the nails indicate a zinc deficiency and nervous strain. Nails take anything up to eight months to grow completely, and are good indicators of present and recent health difficulties. Traditionally, ridges which run down the nails relate to bones or tendons, whilst horizontal ridges relate to shocks to the system, and may indicate nervous difficulties and stresses.

 Caution
As already stated, please be very careful when discussing anything to do with health. Make suggestions or a passing comment, but don't dwell on such matters unless you are medically qualified.

## Practice

We have been looking at minor marks in this chapter, and we are now going to be answering questions on such marks.

• You are looking at a hand with an island in the middle of the Life Line. What would this suggest?

• There is a grille marking on the Jupiter Mount. What does this mean?

• What is the difference between the Psychic Cross and a cross normally found?

• What does it mean when there is a star at the end of the Fate Line?

• There is a star on the Saturn Mount. What does this indicate about the person?

• Where would you expect to find the Teacher's Square?

• Someone seems anxious, and also has a broken Girdle of Venus. What does this indicate about their emotional life?

# CHAPTER 7 – Timings and Compatibilities

In this chapter we will be looking more deeply at the timing of events and/or the age of a person when an event is likely to take place. We will also take a look at compatibilities, and work on a couple of 'real' hands. Timing in particular can be more than a little difficult to gauge correctly. Compatibilities are another area where there may be problems. Make sure you fully understand these sections before making hard and fast statements. It is much better to generalise on these points. Before undertaking an actual palm reading, use the hands given in this chapter and at the end of the book for practice purposes.

## Timing Events

Earlier in this book we took a brief look at the timing of events from the major lines. However, judging age or timing is one of the most difficult areas in palmistry, and there are several methods, or suggested methods, for going about this.

One of the main problems when trying to work out timing is that a very small area, only millimetres in size, covers a year or two in time. It is, therefore, more or less impossible to be precise with the timing of events or suggesting the age of the person at the time of the event. More often than not, even after considerable practice, it is safer to give a time span of about three years either way of the suggested age. Explain to anybody who presses you to give a timing in months, or even weeks, that this is virtually impossible from palmistry alone.

On page 90 is a diagram showing age in relation to the Life, Fate, Success, Head and Heart Lines. Please also bear in mind what was said earlier about timing in the specific sections covering these lines.

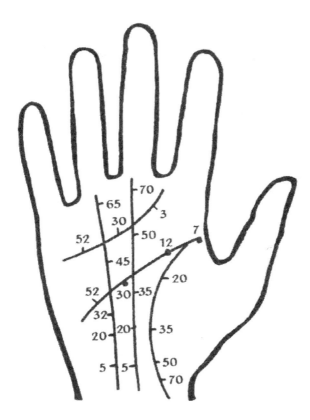

As you will see from the diagram, the Life Line is read downwards, the Fate and Sun Lines are read upwards, and the Head and Heart Lines are read from the thumb side of the palm.

Please note also that not everyone's hand will correspond to the hand shown here; some may be slightly different. For example, the Head Line may be low, the Heart Line may be high or the Life Line may be less curved. Make allowances for these variables.

## Compatibilities

Most people, if they are totally honest, are interested in knowing who they may be compatible with. All of us get on with some people better than with others; sometimes we like a person from the outset, sometimes it is just the opposite and, for no apparent reason, we dislike someone from the first moment we meet them.

Compatibilities are not limited to personal, one-to-one, loving relationships. Compatibilities cover relationships at work, in the social setting, with relatives and so on. They also cover group situations, where we may feel unable to respond well to all the people within a group. However, to assume that there will ever be a situation where everyone gets on with everyone else, whether the group has come together through palmistry suggestions, astrology suggestions or whatever, is totally unrealistic.

There are many reasons why people get on and why they don't. Palmistry can give one explanation, astrology may give another, and psychologists will no doubt give another. However, from looking at hand-types, we may be able to shed more light on the situation.

## Hand Types

At the start of this book, we took a look at hand-types, and gave indications on character from each.

Taking a Square Hand-type as a starting point, and remembering the characteristics of that person will be practicality, orderliness and determination, you can conclude that these people will get on reasonably well with the Active Hand-type.

Conic Hand-types will generally get on well with most people, as they are adaptable and versatile. However, they should get on very well with Psychic Hand-type people.

Psychic Hand-type people, whilst they may get on well with Conic Hand-types, will not get on well with Square or Active Hand-type people. However, they should get on well with the Philosophic Hand-type.

Philosophic Hand-type people should also complement the Square or Active Hand-type people, who will 'earth them' and keep them in touch with reality.

Elementary Hand-type people are rare, but are more likely to get on with others with a similar hand-type or Square or Active Hand-type people.

## Fingers

All these statements about hand-types are generalisations, and to be more certain on compatibilities, we must look at fingers.

Where the fingers lie in relationship to the hand as a whole, and to the thumb in particular, can have great relevance in determining the sort of character a person possesses. It is taking into account the character of the person and then relating it to the character of another person which forms the key to compatibilities.

In general terms, long-fingered people will get on well with other long-fingered people. Short fingers generally show a low self-esteem, lack of confidence or poor self-expression. These people will not feel happy with long-fingered people, who are generally better balanced, more disciplined and more thoughtful. Someone who has a palm which is longer than the length of the fingers is likely to be impulsive and have no interest in detail; such people are unlikely to get on well with long-fingered people.

## Thumbs

A person whose thumb angle from the Jupiter Finger is more than 45 degrees is very self-reliant. Generally speaking, the wider the angle of the thumb from the Jupiter Finger, the more adventurous the person is likely to be. Those with an angle less than 45 degrees are likely to be selfish and blinkered. A person whose thumb seems to fit with their total hand is likely to be more balanced than someone who, for example, has a thumb which seems too heavy for the rest of the hand, and is likely to be very volatile in temperament.

## Lines

Look at the lines on the hand too, and see if there are any similarities between the hand of one person and that of another. If the Head Lines appear to be the same or similar, the two people are likely to think in the same way. However, that does not mean they will necessarily agree on all issues.

Relationships will always involve an element of chance; if we all knew whom we would get on with all the time, life would be very dull.

## Reading a Palm

The next two pages show imprints of two hands. The first hand belongs to a man aged 47, whose job relates to sales and who has been divorced for many years. The second hand belongs to a woman aged 52, who has worked in housing since leaving school, and who married late in life. Take a look at these two right hands for a minute or so.

First Print

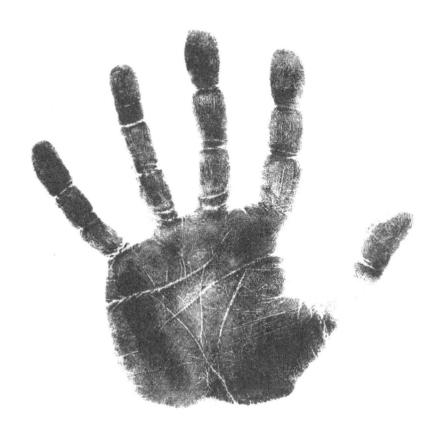

## Second Print

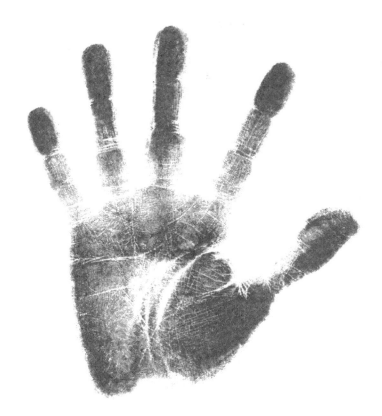

What have you noticed about the two hands? Both people are right-handed incidentally. We have not taken a print of their left hands.

Let's take a look at the first hand. A few pointers will be given here, but it is up to you to do the best you can to produce an assessment.

Pretend the man has come to you for help in his career progression. Note the fact that the Health Line joins the Life Line. Note also that there appears to be part of a Girdle of

Venus visible - the middle may be missing, but the rest is there. There is also a broken Mercury Ring, a tassled end to the Heart Line, the Life Line seems to go into two different directions near the wrist, and the Fate Line, which is very strong, appears to stop at the Heart Line. What assessments would you make from these features? Are there any other signs you can see? What hand-type category would you place this hand in?

Spend as much time as you want to look at this hand before moving on to look at the woman's hand.

The woman concerned has come to you for support. She has had a few worrying health concerns in the last three years, and whilst none of these have been serious, there have been visits to hospitals etc. She has just been promoted at work, and is concerned about meeting the new challenge.

Notice how the Life Line seems to separate around the 40-year mark. Notice also that there appears to be a Line of Mars, the split on the Fate Line and the short Heart Line with a broken end. Note
also the Loyalty Lines, the lines at the base of most, if not all, fingers, Medical Stigmata above the end of the Heart Line, the Travel Lines from the edge of the palm, and in particular the minor marks between the Head and Heart Lines and around the Fate Line. There also appear to be stress lines on the second and third finger phalanges. What other signs can you see? What hand-type category would you place this hand in?

## Reading Hands from Here Onwards

Remember whenever you set out to look at someone's hand. Look closely, with a magnifying glass if possible, and in good, preferably natural light. Make sure your subject is relaxed. Note that how they hold their hands when you are chatting before taking hold of the hand. Maybe also look to see how they hold their hands when they walk into the room.

It is best to see the subject on their own, so you don't have to be careful about what you say, and can be fair and truthful. If the subject is unable to be there in person, make sure they send you a good impression, either a photocopy (several may be best, and make sure you get both hands) or an ink imprint. Remember any imprint you get will be reversed; a right hand will have the thumb shown on the left.

Looking at a palm is a serious business. It is not something you should undertake light-heartedly after a meal or a few drinks. Take your time; be sure you and your subject are comfortable. Try to make sure you won't be disturbed, and that someone is there to answer the telephone (or take it off the hook or use voicemail). If you have children, make sure they have something to do, and are supervised if necessary.

The subject should hold out both hands for inspection. It is a good idea to have something like a small cushion for them to rest their hands upon - holding your hands outstretched without support leads to weary arms and tension.

Having looked at the shape of the hands (the backs and the palms), the fingers and how they lie in relation to the thumb, the colour, the nails, the temperature, then start to look at the lines, mounts and small marks.

Any advice you give should be concise and straightforward. Make sure your subject understands what you are saying, and if necessary explain why you are saying what you are, especially if relating to any timing. Make sure you look at both hands to see the differences, and again explain the differences. Make sure you allow time to answer any questions, and make sure that you are careful over health and relationship issues.

Remember that the lines on your hands change. Professional palmists suggest that the small lines change over a six-month span, so you might suggest to your subject that you would like to look again in six month's time. In such cases, it is interesting to look at health aspects as well as at career and emotional matters.

Look at your own hand too. Perhaps you could take imprints of your own hand over an eighteen-month period, take notes on what changes you have undergone in that period, and then relate these back to the imprints. You may be surprised at what is revealed and how accurate any predictions you made earlier were!

To help you build up your confidence and give you some practice at looking at real hands, I have included some additional palm prints at the end of this book. See how many lines and features you can recognise without referring to the text; then look more closely for the less obvious marks. You'll be surprised just how different hands can be.

Above all, enjoy what you are doing! You will learn a lot about other people, and may also learn something about yourself.

# Further practice Hands

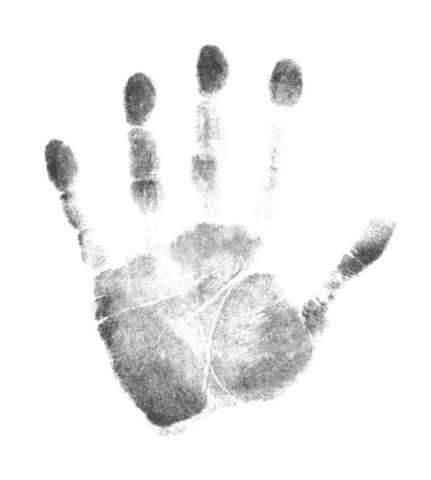

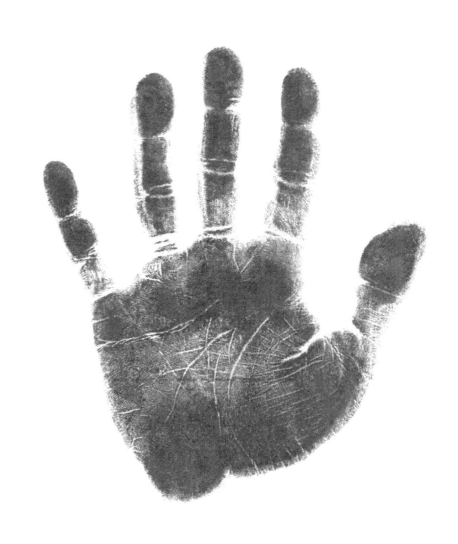

Made in the USA
Middletown, DE
19 August 2017